GRAY ROADS TO GRASS ROOTS

Journey Through Life

GRAY ROADS TO GRASS ROOTS

G Dennis Cantrill

TATE PUBLISHING & Enterprises

Published by Tate Publishing & Enterprises, LLC
127 E. Trade Center Terrace | Mustang, Oklahoma 73064 USA
1.888.361.9473 | www.tatepublishing.com

Tate Publishing is committed to excellence in the publishing industry. The company reflects the philosophy established by the founders, based on Psalm 68:11,
"The Lord gave the word and great was the company of those who published it."

Book design copyright © 2011 by Tate Publishing, LLC. All rights reserved.
Cover design by Joel Uber
Interior design by Sarah Kirchen

Published in the United States of America

ISBN: 978-1-61346-012-2
Biography & Autobiography / Personal Memoirs
11.07.26

This story is dedicated to those who have taken time to visit the back roads of this land and to meet its wonderful people.

ACKNOWLEDGEMENTS

Don White, the retired editor of the Anderson News and author of the Kentucky Traveler columns, who was one of the first to encourage me to complete this story.

Julie Stacy, AP English teacher in Shelby County Schools, who did the first rough and one of the final editings of this book.

My wife and traveling soul mate, Diane, who has been with me every step of the way on this story of *Gray Roads to Grass Roots: Journey Through Life.* It was her encouragement and work along beside me that is a major reason for this completed story. Most of the pictures are those she has accumulated over the years.

Finally, America, which is the real inspiration of the story.

TABLE OF CONTENTS

BEGINNINGS

DECEMBER 20, 1948

On this cold December day a first grader was reluctantly again heading off to school. Okay, there were a couple of things on the bright side. Santa Claus was just five days away. In addition, and maybe more importantly, it was a Christmas break away from Sister Blister. Sister Blister was a six foot nun who could have easily been mistaken for Darth Vader. As a first grade teacher she was the worst nightmare of any normally active six year old boy. She certainly believed in *spare the rod and you spoil the child.* I still feel my knuckles ache. (After all, I was left-handed.)

About two hours after the school day started I saw Mother walking in to the school building. *Oh! Oh!* Did Sister Blister call her? Has something bad happened? A mother showing up at school in midmorning is rarely a good sign, even in the limited experience of a first grader. And if you thought Sister Blister was bad, that was only a fraction of the terror of getting in trouble at school, then having to face my parents at home.

I was the youngest of four boys and sufficiently spoiled because I was the *baby.* However, I never had a chance. My older brothers had done whatever could be done at some time or the other. My parents definitely had a defined no-tolerance policy when it came to our behavior at school.

I'M THE CUTE ONE IN FRONT

ON WITH THE STORY

I meekly followed my mother out of school and to the waiting car. Guess what? My dad and brothers were waiting for us there. Now I was confused. Something terrible must have happened for my whole family to be loaded up in the middle of a weekday morning. When I asked, as a six-year-old might, my mother said, "We are going for a trip." I had not heard a word about any trip. I think they sent me to school that day just to keep me out of the way (smart move).

I immediately wanted to know, "Where are we going?" Mother explained that we were going to visit her brother, my uncle Charley, in Texas City, Texas for Christmas! *What? Not at home for Christmas?*

Then it hit me. Not at home for Christmas! It was then that my egocentric personality of the time reared its ugly head—to paraphrase in grown up terms, "How the hell is Santa Claus ever going to find me in Texas? This is the dumbest damn idea yet!" Even thoughts of having escaped Sister Blister never entered my mind. At that point real panic hit, and the whining, crying, and gnashing of teeth began in earnest. All this was to no avail, except to increase the laughter of my three older brothers.

Oh, but as always Mother came to the rescue as she informed me that Santa Claus had been told where we would be for Christmas and not to worry. *Okay,* mothers do *not* lie.

That night while unloading the luggage, as a normally inquisitive six-year-old might, I noticed *hidden* packages in the trunk. Having caused enough trouble for almost four hundred and forty miles, I thankfully kept my mouth shut, for once (before Dad really noticed me). On Christmas morning at my uncle's house, those same packages showed up under the tree from Santa Claus. It was at that point that I gave credibility to my older brothers who had cruelly let me know that there really was not a real Santa Claus. However, I managed to pretend for many years afterwards that I was still a true believer.

THAT FIRST TRIP

Being born in August of 1942, I was a prelude to most of what are called Baby Boomers. With three older brothers, and the one next to me almost six years older, I have often thought of myself as a mistake. Just maybe it was one hell of a Christmas or New Year's Eve party. The timing is right, so it would make my conception around Christmas or New Year's.

What does this have to do with the first trip? Not a darn thing, except I want to set the era in which that first trip occurred. For my older brothers World War II was very real. The war was a time when we rationed food and fuel, there were no new cars and tires, and many other things taken for granted today just were not available. There was almost no travel for pleasure. I even still have some ration stamps that permitted my parents to buy food for me.

I can only imagine how happy and proud my family was when we got a new Buick Road Master and actually could buy enough gasoline to take a trip for a vacation. In later life, I found out that in the years prior to World War II my family had traveled to several places, but all that had come to a halt for the years during the war. Dad had even pulled an old Teardrop trailer to Florida and had camped on the Tamiami Trail in the mid-1930s, and my brothers had visited such places as Monticello, Washington DC, Atlantic City, Smokey Mountains, and more. Therefore, road trips were a family tradition I had never experienced. This was to be my first.

Traveling in a car with my dad was an experience. First, he really enjoyed driving and secondly, he was a good driver.

Although he had a heavy foot and always *tried out* a new car, he never had an accident in almost seventy years of driving. He covered a lot of ground, and many years, with his construction work, he drove over one hundred thousand miles. Even into his eighties I would ride with him and think just how good of a driver he really was. As my maternal grandmother would say, "I don't really like riding in cars, but I would ride through hell with Curtis."

So that day was my first real road-trip experience. I do remember parts of the trip, but some details about the trip come from stories by Dad, my brothers, old photographs, and even some from my very faint memories. However, most of the facts come from a log my mother kept in a small notebook. I found it when cleaning out personal effects after my father's death. She kept, not a diary, but a true log of several of the trips we took. It included notes on routes, mileage, and time driven, as well as fuel, food, and lodging cost. After seeing this, my wife Diane thought it was such a great idea that she has kept a very similar log. We often refer to it when revisiting an area—whether to pick out a good campsite, a motel, a good place to eat, or avoid a bad road—and yes, to rekindle memories.

FINALLY ON THE ROAD

Leaving our then hometown of Middlesboro, Kentucky, at mid-morning on today's interstates with a man who drove fast, you would expect to get a long way. Well, we made it all the way to Birmingham, Alabama, even on the old roads. Staying at my first hotel was quite an experience. Actually, about all I remember is being in trouble, because I was adamant that the only thing I wanted for supper was a peanut butter and jelly sandwich.

The next day we headed south through Alabama and Mississippi to Biloxi. I do remember my first glimpses of cotton fields, and it was that night I got to see the ocean for the first time. We stayed at the Edgewater Gulf Hotel that was then, and the last time I was there a few years ago, a pretty good hotel. Sadly, the hotel was destroyed during Hurricane Katrina. Other than the ocean, what I remember most was dinner, a peanut butter and jelly sandwich, and pushing back my chair and turning it over in this fancy dining room. Not hurt, I still had managed to show my ass again. Why they didn't drop me off the balcony or take me out to sea and leave is still a mystery. By the way, the bill from room for two adults, four children, dinner, hotel, and gas that day totaled twenty-eight dollars, and we drove over four hundred miles. Note: My eight-year-old grandson got his first look and walk on an ocean beach with me at the same place in 2009 some sixty-one years later.

From Biloxi we headed west along US Highway 90 to New Orleans. Having driven this route several times over the years, it has retained much of the same character with bays, bayous, fishing villages, and swamps. This is in spite of new Casinos, condominiums, and hurricanes.

What do I remember most about that first visit to New Orleans? In my six-year-old mind, it was the guide Dad hired to show us around the city. I still have never again seen such a mustache on a woman. Strange what a kid remembers isn't it? I also remember Dad almost calling off the tour when she insisted she would drive the new car because the streets were narrow and hard to find.

Of course, I think my oldest brother Charles always remembered Pat O'Brien's as his name was over the door, Charlie Cantrell (a part owner). I think, after being old enough, he returned to meet the owner and partake of the local libations, maybe even to excess. Pat O'Brien's is the home of the original hurricane. I still consider New Orleans one of my favorite places, even though I generally do not like most cities. The next few days are a blur of memories that included: fighting with my cousins, sleeping with several in a bed, having a Christmas with heat and sand, and seeing the results of the great 1947 explosion in Texas City. There were actually steel scraps in my uncle's yard. Of course, the packages from Santa Claus did find their way to Texas. Will miracles never cease?

As we headed on west, one of my most vivid memories is San Antonio and the Alamo. San Antonio has become one of my more favorite places to revisit. The River Walk, the markets, the food and music, while of a much different heritage, are much like New Orleans. I sure would not want to live there but do enjoy a day or so just because it is not a typical American city.

Hey, I said Dad liked to drive and had a heavy foot, so we next ended up in El Paso after a night in Alpine. Much of west Texas was spent on the road in combat (I usually lost) with my older brothers, who I sometimes derived great pleasure in making extremely miserable. Nothing like being a younger brother who causes trouble then runs to Mom. (That takes talent in a car at 70 mph.) El Paso was my first real glimpse of Mexican culture, especially when we crossed over to Juarez. What impressed me most? Why, the sombreros, of course! Now, later in life, I find the senoritas much more impressive.

Still heading west to Arizona, I have retained two or three cherished memories of that state, such as: one brother tricking another into backing into a cactus while taking his picture, visiting the Petrified Forest when you could still just pick up a souvenir—thankfully there are some still left, and we know better now or nothing would be left—and driving the steep hills of Jerome.

Last of all, the thing that really set my course, and is the first source of my insatiable appetite to see it all, was that first view of the Grand Canyon. Even though just six years old, I knew I was standing on the edge of one of creation's greatest wonders. It was almost beyond belief. I have visited several times since and remain awestruck at its grandeur. No pictures or words are sufficient to duplicate the feeling when you first walk to the canyon edge. In later years, I have returned with my wife, my children, my grandchildren, and my friends. When I go now, at first I really try not to linger by looking into the canyon, but rather I watch their faces. Nothing is more rewarding than seeing their expressions, knowing that they feel a lot like I did many years ago.

This was the beginning, and I can't say Grand Canyon is my most favorite place to visit, but it was really the first. It was kind of like the first time you made love. It may not remain the best or the most memorable, but it retains a cherished place in your mind.

HEADING HOME

At about two o'clock in the morning, while sleeping peacefully, I was rudely awakened. I am sure I blurted out questions and comments such as:

"Huh, what is going on?"

"We are leaving?"

"Why?"

"It is snowing?"

"All right! Snow!"

Nope, there was to be no playing in snow at Grand Canyon. Many untold miles later I have my next memory of staying the night, and it was not snowing anymore. Did we stop? I have no idea, and Mother's log was pretty incoherent about this period. Dad, in later years, would only say that he wanted to stay ahead of the storm, and he did. What I really think now is they didn't want a snow to delay getting me back into the clutches of Sister Blister.

This was the first of many trips I took with my parents. However, it was the only one that the whole family ever took together. My oldest brother, Charles, was off to college, followed shortly thereafter by Jim. I look back on this trip, and while memories are hazy, I know this was something that planted a seed in my soul.

AMERICA THE BEAUTIFUL

O beautiful for spacious skies,
For amber waves of grain,
For purple mountains majesty
Above the fruited plains!
America! America!
God shed his grace on thee
And crown thy good with brotherhood
From sea to shining sea!

—Words by Katherine Lee Bates,
Music by Samuel Ward

These words bring back memories and a special feeling I have developed about my journeys throughout this land in a lifetime of travel. Yet as I have worked through the writing of my story, it became apparent that neither words nor even pictures could really capture the essence of this awesome place. Most of my lifetime exploring the back roads as well as the main roads has been like a journey through life.

Why *Gray Roads to Grass Roots:* Journey Through Life? The title was originally *Gray Roads and Gluttony* and comes from planning a trip in 2007 with my daughter and her family. I knew our routes would often follow several roads that are shown in gray on many maps, and some are not even on most maps. Stealing an idea from one of my favorite books *Blue Highways* by Least Heat Moon, I came up with *gray roads* as a partial name for this family tour. It was also appropriate as we were going to be in Chase County, Kansas, which also was written about by that author in *PrairyErth*.

The *gluttony* part was because on this tour we would be visiting places I had traveled through many times to visit ranches and buy cattle. In some of these small towns, I had been introduced to some of the best cafes and steakhouses in the nation. The food was good enough to tempt you to gluttony. And if I was going to write my story, it had to have a title.

When considering a final title for my story I didn't want the reader to think that the gluttony part was a negative thing. Therefore the final title has ended up being *Gray Roads to Grass Roots: Journey Through Life*. This title actually sums up better what my story is all about.

A couple of years ago my Aunt Thelma showed me some of my grandfather Cantrell's writings about things in his life in the early 1900s. Even though it was short, I thought that a story by my grandfather about his early life was quite an inheritance. If I could put together a collection of stories about my journeys through life, just maybe I could leave an enduring inheritance to my children and grandchildren.

SOME SAMPLES FROM
MY GRANDFATHER

Writing about school:

> The fountain of knowledge is greater than we know, greater than our understanding permits, greater than even the brightest minds of all time can comprehend.

Remembering happy school days:

> It is unfortunate that the happiness of the day has to dim in later life. We slept then, dreamed that life was beautiful, and awoke to find that life is duty. Duty and love are bound in a common tie, no force of evil can sever it, and forces for good strengthen it materially.

Describing his nine-mile route across the mountains to where he went to high school, boarding during the week:

> It was five miles climb up to the state line over a rough trail. The lofty trees cast a beautiful shade and the giant sized rocks marked our roadway like today's road signs. The trail on both sides of the gap is like a never ending Z. Passing this way often I will never forget the markings on the route, a beautiful field first left then right, a giant tree here and another there, a towering cliff in the hazy distance standing as sentinel to the entire countryside.

My grandfather went on to become a respected teacher for several years, followed by many years as a postmaster.

After reading what my grandfather had written I began to think about trying to write my story. When I looked at the tour title of Gray Roads and Gluttony for our 2007 tour, a light bulb appeared on top of my head. This was it! A beginning! That title really summed up the story I wanted to tell.

By the way, we still have not made the Gray Roads and Gluttony tour. Instead of heading west, we did a complete 180-degree change in direction less than twenty-four hours before we planned to leave. Gray Roads and Gluttony became Cruising and Clam Cakes for this year, but that is for a story later on.

Huh? You name your trips? Yep, doesn't everybody call his vacation or trip something? How many times have you heard them say my Florida vacation, fall foliage tour, European trip, Gatlinburg shopping, or any number of countless other titles? However, I usually wanted to be just a little different in how I perceived and remembered my travels. Even if it did not have a name before we left, it did by the time we got home. The titles weren't always really creative or unusual, but I tried.

Another thing that I often do is have a written plan, even if we do not follow it, and I had to title it something. However, sometimes I just like to leave, and as the old saying goes, "follow my nose." With a wife and traveling partner who must be fully informed as to the appropriate wardrobe to take, that is not always the easiest thing to accomplish. I discovered several years ago that, unless Diane was fully informed, a long bed, double cab pickup truck would not hold what showed up when we loaded. Like a boy scout, her motto is, "Be prepared," and she would be *fully*.

THE HARD PART

I have always enjoyed telling or listening to a story, especially when I have the option of stretching the truth (just a little) and have no limit on the length. My motto is to never let the absolute facts get in the way of a good story. The hard part is telling it so even those of us with short attention spans get the point and our minds do not wander.

In starting this book, I recalled what a former vice president from Kentucky, Alben Barkley, said when ask about giving a speech: "If you want me to give a five minute speech it will take several days to prepare, but if I have hours to talk I am ready now" (paraphrased, but you get the idea). Therefore, I hope I can tell my story completely without hearing too many snores.

ABOUT THE BOOK

This story is a combination of travel stories, but not a travel guide; journeys through life, but not a biography; it is a little philosophy and a few lame attempts at humor. When reading what I have written, a conclusion of mine is that this story is really like me, pretty good at several things but not really great at anything.

A note on my humor: many of my attempts are a poke at me. Over the years I have developed a philosophy: I take my family, my job, and my life seriously, but I really try not to take myself too seriously. However, sometimes my humor attempts can sometimes be best described as *foot in mouth.*

While many people play golf, have a boat, or have a host of other escapes from the real world, I have my journeys. After all, as Least Heat Moon says, "There are no yesterdays on the road."

In starting this story, there was really no point or conclusion intended. Most of all, it was an attempt to leave memories for family and friends, even if I have not met them yet.

However, reflecting on what I had written, there emerged a hope that those who have the patience to read this story do develop a desire to see more than just the high profile tourist spots or the same place with people just like themselves over and over. . Maybe after people have read this it might be a motivation to try a few *Gray Roads* on their own journeys. This is a wonderful country with beautiful vistas, nooks, and crannies filled with interesting people, but it can't really be experienced from an interstate, a tourist resort, from forty thousand feet, or even a guided tour.

Another hope of mine is that at least a few of my readers will be inspired to someday sit down and tell their own story—whether written or recorded in their own words, their thoughts, feelings, and life experiences are a priceless heritage.

ABOUT THE TRAVELS

In my lifetime, I have visited every state but Alaska (I will get there sometime), along with seven Canadian provinces and three Mexican states, Many of these states have been visited several times. And almost every trip taken has, at least in part, been a road trip at some point. I have rarely just gone someplace and stayed put. There is some built-in urge to explore.

It is my belief that even if I am going to someplace specific, that quite often what I see and do getting there is just as important as getting there—to me that is kind of like life itself.

In writing this book, one thing I did was to get a road atlas and highlight all the roads and routes I remembered. Most states look like they have been infested with spider veins. Something that I have discovered about myself is that somehow I have developed a unique ability to remember routes, places, and things I have seen. It is almost like there is a photograph embedded in my mind—certainly not important, but it is there.

Also in writing this book I have come to the conclusion that while I have been a lot of places and seen a lot of things, there will never be enough time or money to see and do all that I would like to, let alone revisit everywhere I would like to.

ABOUT KENTUCKY

In this story a notable absence is references to travels in my home state, Kentucky. There are two reasons for this: first of all, they could almost fill another book, and secondly, that leaves a future writing project.

Kentucky is about as beautiful and diverse as any place in the USA. It has mountains, rolling hills, caves, flat lands, and the rolling bluegrass that I call home. The Native Americans considered it a sacred hunting ground.

FALL ON THE FARM

In my lifetime, though I could not swear to it, I believe that at some point in time I have visited all one hundred and twenty counties. Many were visited with my dad in his road construction business, or showing cattle at county fairs, and often just short jaunts for a couple of days to see something that I had not seen before.

SOME PHILOSOPHY

In the "Beginnings" I finished up with how that first trip was a spark to start a journey to *see it all.* But it did more than just get me hooked on the great things; it started a journey toward looking for more—more of this wonderful country, the unique fascinating people who live here, and of course, meals beyond peanut butter and jelly.

As much as I hate to admit it, I am biased. Those who have not seen the expansive beauty of our nation's highways and byways or become fascinated with its cultural diversity are truly deprived. To me they are like the little kid at the parade standing behind an adult. They are there; they can hear the music, but they have a very limited view of what a parade really is about. (Think about what they see.)

Anyone with even basic financial ability almost has a duty to see this wonderful land and its people. I have met lots of people who say they do travel, but in reality the only thing they have ever done is drive an interstate at over 70 mph, often in the middle of the night with a view of the rear-end of a semi, or be lined up to get on a plane to see the USA from forty thousand feet. They are on their way for a week at the beach, skiing, Disney World, or shopping in some big city. Far too many people think that travel has to be to a high profile, often expensive, place, but I am living proof that great journeys can be made with little funds beyond the everyday cost of living.

Like many people I have spent a week at the beach, visited Disney World and Disney Land, and on rare occasions been conned into going shopping. However, from my perspective, I would be very much like the kid standing behind an adult at a parade if that was all I had done.

Other people can talk about their world travels and the cities and continents they have visited. At one time I had ambitions to be a world traveler. However, as time has passed, I have come to the reality that not only will I never have the money to be a world traveler, but definitely will run out of time before I have been able to see and do all I want to right here at home.

So when getting a little down because I never have or never will be a world traveler, I think, *Yep, that's neat. But have they ever been to the Fourth of July celebration at the Crawford, Nebraska rodeo or Gorham, New Hampshire fair, or eaten lunch at the liars' table with the cowboys at Cassoday Café? Did they ever sit miles from anywhere on top of the Bighorn Mountains and watch moose graze? Or sit cuddled up, as I have alone with my wife, on a hilltop in Nova Scotia overlooking the Atlantic, and been one of the first people in North America to see the sun come up? And I'd bet most never sat on the stage at a Shakespearean play in Chicago.*

While appreciating many of the things people usually see and do, I also have a desire to find places and do things beyond the obvious that many people may miss, and find great pleasure in doing so.

SOME BACKGROUND

I was raised in a family that had above-average income, but was not rich. My dad, as a chemical engineer and later as a successful road contractor, made good money, and we were able to travel. This was especially true for me as the youngest. By the time I became a teenager, we also had a large registered Angus herd of cattle. I took several trips with my parents to cattle shows, sales, and ranch visits in conjunction with the herd.

However, I have never been as successful financially as my parents were. Most of my adult life, while not in poverty, I would classify my status as independently poor.

While this status has limited the use of upscale hotels, resorts, and restaurants, it has never deterred the travel. In fact, I feel that this less-than-abundant financial situation has made me a more creative traveler. I have always tried to travel *on the cheap*. It often amazes people who have traveled with me that I find really good, inexpensive places to stay, eat, or visit.

Now that the stage is set, the balance of this story is about journeys through a lifetime. Along the way will be trips, places to eat that can tempt you to gluttony, neat places to stay, some interesting people and a few funny happenings, And my personal *journey through life*.

TRAVELS WITH GRANDMAS

ME (THE TOUR GUIDE) AND MY GRANDMAS

For a few years after the Beginnings trip, travel with my parents was limited to annual winter dashes to Florida, usually over Christmas. Dad was busy establishing an asphalt paving company that took what seemed like twenty-four hours a day in the summer, and I was firmly entrenched in school in winter. By the way, I finally escaped Sister Blister in the third grade.

At eleven years old another memorable trip occurred early in 1954, a trip with both of my grandmothers. Both of my grandmothers were widows, with Dad's mom being just recently widowed, and she was spending quite a lot of time with us during that period. I still don't know what prompted his decision (I never did with my dad) to gather the grandmas, take me out of school, and head to Florida. But we did.

My grandmothers did not know how fortunate they were. They were to be accompanied by the best guide to Florida they could have. After all, I had been there five times and knew it all.

Now you have to understand, both my grandmothers were the babies in their family, and I was the baby in mine. Talk about a special bond. They knew the truth. The baby was always the best looking and brightest in the family.

I really couldn't give an exact itinerary, but can piece a lot together from mom's log—old pictures of me and the grandmas in the carriage at St Augustine, on the beach in big coats, and Silver Springs.

One special memory was at the expense of my dad's mother. She had raised cattle, milked cows, and farmed all her life. One evening we had a not-very-good steak dinner. The next day she saw Brahma cattle for the first time and thought they were the ugliest cows she had ever seen. It was then my sometimes-warped sense of humor kicked in. I said, "Grandma, you know that steak you had last night was from the hump on those cows." There followed a lengthy discussion where I maintained that it was absolutely, no-doubt-about-it true that the steak had come

from the hump. She just acted as if she believed me; however, she laughingly told that story many times over.

Like the Beginnings, that was the first and last travels with both the grandmas. But that ten-day trip remains
special in my mind; even though I later spent time with
both, we never traveled all together again. Another thing
it did was plant another seed.

I joked I was their guide and even thought like it at
the time. It was then I first noticed a look in their eyes. It
was a look I have noticed over the years in many people. It
is a look of wonder or joy or awe. They saw the ocean, saw
an alligator, and saw swamps and Spanish moss. In addition, Grandma saw her first Brahma cow.

COW DROPPINGS

For several years, many travels, other than our annual dash to Florida, involved our cattle herd when we traveled. There were many trips around the Midwest, to Shenandoah Valley, and to shows, sales, and conferences all over the country. Most do not really bring back too many travel memories, but occasionally there are things that stand out in my mind—often these involve people as much as places.

In the registered cattle business you can interact with the whole spectrum of people in the United States from farmers to rich and famous, corporate CEOs, even a US President. When I was fifteen we were looking for some particular imported Scottish bloodlines. An auction just on the north side of Chicago near Forest Park was advertised featuring those bloodlines.

When we got to the farm, it wasn't a farm; it was an *estate*. While not poor, I would now say I got to see how the wealthy live. The almost one hundred-foot buffet for dinner was impressive, but not what made this memorable. It was what happened at dinner that really sticks in my mind. Being an almost normal fifteen-year-old boy, it was not unusual that, unless required to and given a choice, you do not sit with your parents, and I didn't. Getting my plate, I approached a table some distance away. About the same time as I sat, a man about my dad's age was sitting down across from me. We struck up a conversation.

He was from Texas. His name was Ed. We talked cows, family, and other things. He was one of the most personable men I have met. Going along I could feel my ego increasing (a real grownup conversation). After a while I inquired if he, like my dad, had other interest besides ranching. Yes, he did have a small general merchandise store. As our conversation was ending, I asked his full name. His reply—Edward Marcus. (Do you know where I am going yet?)

As we returned to the hotel, I was telling Dad about the really nice man I had met—how he ranched and had a small general store and all. Just as soon as I told him that his name was Edward Marcus, Dad almost wrecked from laughing so hard. He proceeded to inform me that this small general merchandise store was the second largest in the world, Neiman Marcus. And I had no place to hide.

The next day I was almost embarrassed to talk with Mr. Marcus again. Why worry? Deep in my mind, I wondered if, bluntly speaking, he thought I was just a full of BS kid. I resembled that sometimes. All's well that ends well. I must have not done all that badly. At our next annual sale, although he couldn't make it himself, he sent a bid that purchased our top selling animal. The next year, when my parents visited in Texas, he gave them a personal tour of the small general merchandise store and flew them out to see his ranch.

This incident set me on a course to never again try to impress anybody with my own importance. Over the years, I have worked to feel comfortable whether talking with a national leader, corporate giant, a field hand, or even having a beer with an off duty, beat-cop in Laredo, Mexico. Each person in his own way adds to the fabric of life.

People are as interesting as any magnificent scenery or painting—each adds to the landscape of life and to you. Like someone who has seen the parade but never heard the music, something is missing. If you only have conversations with friends, people in your social class, or those who you are comfortable with, you have limited yourself and your growth.

KISS GEORGE ON THE NOSE

As I said earlier, my family prospered in both the road construction and cattle business. So for a man who liked to travel, Dad's next step was to get an airplane. It was a single engine Cessna 175, and later a push-pull twin Cessna 335.

The summer between one of my multiple attempts at a college education (I was invited to leave occasionally) the National Angus Conference was to be held in Great Falls, Montana. So Dad, who never planned a trip too far ahead, decided we should fly out to it, leaving tomorrow. There was unusual weather for mid-July with the passage of a cold front and beautiful clear skies. We took off from Lexington, Kentucky, where we then lived, and flew at the low altitude of fifteen hundred feet to Pierre, South Dakota for a night stop. Seeing the Midwest from that low of an altitude is not quite like driving the gray roads, but almost as good.

Early the next morning we took off to head on to Great Falls and in-route plan a close fly-by of Mount Rushmore. (Probably can't do that anymore.) We did a really neat fly-by with a couple of passes. One of which was close up! Looking around, I saw that my mother's face was almost as white as a sheet.

Now Mom was never a good flyer, but she hung in pretty well, knowing it was either fly or get left home. Worried, I asked if she was okay. When she nodded to the affirmative, I returned to the scenery. After clearing the mountains, I looked back to see her whispering in Dad's ear. And immediately the whole plane was filled with his laughter. What is going on? After a few minutes waiting for him to quit laughing, I found out.

Mother had said to him, "We flew so close I could have kissed George Washington on the nose. *Do not do that again!*"

On this trip, I was introduced to the wonders of Glacier National Park, which will also figure in a later story. Glacier is another one of the places I consider *creation's greatest wonders*. While visiting a few times later in life, I only stayed in the Many Glacier and Prince of Wales Lodges this one time. The stay in these lodges made a lasting impression on me.

TWO BOYS WEST!

The flying trip to the National Angus Conference in Montana was not my first introduction to the Great Plains and Rocky Mountains—that happened in 1959 when I was sixteen years old. Both my brother Bill and I worked hard on the farm in the hay fields and with the cattle. Usually our days started before six in the morning and ended at dark, sometimes later. It was a normal summer to get all the routine chores done, show cattle, bale thirty thousand bales of hay, and do that much more custom hay baling for other people.

In early July, we had been discussing that we would like to see the West, visit some ranches and Yellowstone, and more. So we approached Dad, asking if we could take a break and make a trip out west. I guess I shouldn't have been surprised and wouldn't be now, but he gave his blessing. So we loaded up Mother's 1955 Super 98 Oldsmobile and headed west, complete with camping stuff and all.

At that time there were almost no interstate highways, only two-lane roads. Adrenaline-pumped with excitement, I think we left at three in the morning because we couldn't sleep. At Louisville we picked up US Highway 150 and followed it in the dark to US 50 at Shoals, Indiana, then on to Saint Louis. I don't remember where we stayed, but before noon the next day we were in northwest Missouri.

There we had our first real stop at the JCPenney Farm near Cameron, Missouri, known as Home Place Farm. We didn't get to meet Mr. Penney, but had a great visit with his manager, Orin James. Later that year we bought a bull, Homeplace Eileenmere 863, that we saw on our stop there. He was purchased when JC Penney Farm exhibited him at the National Angus Futurity. The Futurity was held, at that time, at Keeneland Race Track in Lexington, Kentucky. This bull proved to be a good herd bull for us.

After a couple of more farm visits in that area, we headed on west on US 36. To this day I still can't identify with people that tell me, "Kansas is just flat—nothing to see and boring." They have never taken the time to look (more on Kansas later).

To a farm boy the long rolling hills of alfalfa and wheat fields in northern Kansas, along with beehives that were being hauled on trucks to pollinate alfalfa for seed, were fascinating. The miles rolled by with new sights over every hill. And we got to stand at the geographical center of the lower forty-eight states. In fact, we spent the night nearby at Smith Center.

Finally, we entered Colorado. Anyone who drives west in to Colorado will at first think they are just seeing some distant clouds. But finally, you come to the realization that it is the snow-covered peaks of the Rockies. Everybody should make their first trip to the Rockies driving across the high, dry plains of northeastern Colorado.

We followed US 36 on to Denver, but now my favorite way is up through Sterling, Colorado and across Highway 14. This route takes you through the high plains wheat fields, and you can actually look at the scenery and not the back-end of a semi. It also lets your mind wander back to how the first settlers may have felt. You are rolling along at a high speed, covering more miles in an hour than they usually did maybe in weeks, yet you think it takes a long time to get to the mountains.

From Denver we headed toward Rocky Mountain National Park. Oh, boy! Camping in the Rockies! However, that was not to be. Stopping at the now-gone Trail Ridge Ranch (I think that was the name) for lunch, as we really could not cook much more than a can of beanie weenies or Spam anyway, we found out that rooms were available for a couple of nights. Although a little pricey at eight dollars a night for the two of us, we decided to splurge.

The next day yielded one of the great adventures of my young life. There was a trail ride from the lodge up to the top of Fall River Pass. While US 34 goes to the top we rode the original gravel trail that was too narrow for a vehicle. It has since become a one lane road up.

Up and up we rode to the 11,796-foot pass, stopping in a flat just short of where the visitor center now stands. It had taken all of the morning to wind up the switchbacks, riding beside thousand-foot drop-offs and thoroughly enjoying the awesome vistas (and views of the tight jeans of the young ladies with us).

At our stop there was a packed lunch for us, oats for the horses, and a break for our legs. Both of us had ridden for many years and were in good shape from all the farm work, but crawling off the horses, we could barely walk.

After the lunch break and a snowball fight, we headed back down. Following us from the west was a large dark cloud. Soon there came up a cold wind followed by hail, light rain, and snow flurries. Thankfully, we found out that in the rain-shadow of the mountains, outfitters always packed slickers for the riders. We didn't end up too chilled or looking like drowned rats; in fact, we were barely dampened, and our spirits certainly weren't. That night both of us had leg cramps, but to this day, I can't say for sure if it was the riding or dancing with the tight jeans that night.

After another full day of exploring the park, it was westward ho we go. The day started early enough to reach the top of Fall River Pass to see the sunrise from the mountaintops, then down through Granby and breakfast at a small place in Hot Sulfur Springs. Little did I know that some twenty-seven years later I would discover one of the great breakfast places in the country just seventeen miles west.

LONE MOOSE CAFÉ

Some twenty-seven years after the Two Boys trip, my wife, Diane, and two of our sons were camping in Rocky Mountain National Park at Timber Creek campground. That Sunday morning had dawned at twenty-six degrees

Fahrenheit in July. Quickly packing up after only coffee, we picked up US 40 at Granby and headed west. It was in my mind to eat breakfast at Hot Sulfur Springs where my brother and I had so many years before. Nothing was open that morning. As we rolled in to Kremmling on US 40 it was the same story, nothing seemed to be open.

However, all was not lost. Glancing up a side street, I spied several pickup trucks parked near the end of the block. That many trucks and not yet time for church on a Sunday morning could only mean a couple of things: either they thought it was still Saturday night, or food.

We walked in to a place with neat Rocky Mountain west décor, complete with a moose head over the bar. What food! The biggest plate of pancakes I have ever seen and the best homemade cinnamon rolls, done right. We knew we had eaten. A few years later in the early 90s on one of our cattlemen's tours, I had it set up to again have breakfast at the Lone Moose Café. Yep, it was still great, and not just because we were hungry on a cold morning.

A tip: one of the best indicators of a place that is highly likely to have great blue-plate food is the number of pickup trucks parked outside. Almost for sure, a place without any trucks will not be good.

■

After passing through the first mountains ranges, there was an introduction to the high, dry, intermountain-grazing lands. For some boys from Kentucky, it was hard to understand how their cattle made it in such an environment of scattered grasses and scrub. And it seemed that after seeing something in the distance it would take forever to reach.

Passing by the Strawberry Reservoir, we reached what I still consider a neat town. Heber City was and is a pretty town nestled in a valley of the dry mountains of Utah. The small towns in Utah can be a real contrast to the starkness of the surrounding mountains. At that time, green lawns were watered from small curbside irrigation ditches, and flowers were everywhere. We were fascinated by the irrigation canals and ditches running around the hills and out in to the valleys and throughout the towns.

The next morning, it was on to see the Great Salt Lake and, of course, drive the Bonneville Salt Flats. I don't remember how it was done, but somehow I convinced big brother Bill it was my turn to drive. A few miles out on the straight, flat road, he dozed off. I thought, *Now's my chance!* Who would have thought that Mom's old Oldsmobile would do 120 mph?

It must have been the wind noise or the rocking, but Bill woke up while we were still doing over 100 mph. After that I didn't get to drive for another two days. The need to see just what a car can do must be genetic.

After entering Nevada, we turned north to Twin Falls, Idaho, and then east on US 20. Had we known it, there were some great views of the Snake River, the falls, and the springs coming out of the side of the canyon there. But we were on the road, so after nearly five hundred miles (almost a fourth during the hour my brother slept), we stopped in another one of my favorite small towns in the west, Rexburg, Idaho.

Rexburg has been a stopover for me several times over the years. While, like many small towns, it is losing the downtown, and local businesses are struggling, it seems to retain much of the charm of that first visit. Surrounded by cropland with potatoes, wheat, soybeans, and more, it is an agricultural based town with a friendly atmosphere. If ever there, head up on to the mountain bench just to the east and you will be almost in the shadow of the Tetons and can overlook the town and see way beyond to the west.

Next, we headed in to what is another one of creation's greatest treasures, Yellowstone National Park. While not as awesome at first sight as the Grand Canyon, the fascination grows. As we entered the park from the west, that first drive up the valley to the lower, midway, and upper geyser basins was a trip of wonder. We not only stopped and walked each one, but also revisited all of them over the next few days.

Arriving at Old Faithful, we got there just minutes before an eruption. And whenever we were not exploring other parts of the park, it seemed Old Faithful was not just faithful, but working overtime. Little did we know then, that just days after we left would come the earthquake that would change Old Faithful to this day.

Since that time, it has never been quite as regular or gone quite as high as it did prior to the big earthquake in 1959. During our stay, all of the geysers were in overdrive. It seemed as if almost all were constantly erupting. I remember being in the upper basin, and it looked like every geyser was going off at the same time.

Again, we had planned to camp in Yellowstone, but when we found that there was a cabin open at six dollars a night where we could just look out and see Old Faithful, we forgot the camping. The park has changed over the years. The crowds have grown, the roads are crowded, and where you can go has become more limited. No longer is it often you can just drive in and get a room without reservations, or as Old Faithful erupts be joined by only a few dozen people.

But that is all right. It is a place that each American should visit at least once in their life. If you don't appreciate the power of the earth and the wonders of creation after visiting Yellowstone, there is little hope for you anyway.

For many people a visit to Yellowstone is just a quick trip to see Old Faithful, Yellowstone Falls, and Mammoth Hot Springs, then and back to more civilized places. (I have been guilty of that.) During that first visit my brother and I spent almost five days exploring both the high spots and back roads of the park. I have come to the conclusion that after having visited, at last count, eleven times, I still have not really explored Yellowstone Park. It is still possible to have a little of the old feeling. In July 2006, when I took my oldest grandchildren there, we were able to recapture some of the same feelings I had experienced years before. Despite their protest, we rolled out before first light and made our way to see Old Faithful erupt. Nothing was open, not even for coffee, but at that almost-predawn eruption, we were joined by no more than a handful of people. The day before there had been thousands standing several deep to get a look. Guess the early bird still gets the worm, so to speak.

EARLY MORNING AT OLD FAITHFUL

No visit to Yellowstone is complete without some reflection. You are standing in a super volcano's caldera. This volcano is so large and powerful that a major top-blowing event could not only devastate much of North America, but threaten all life in the world. The realization that we, as humans, are just a tick in the time clock of the earth makes it worth the trip. Most often, we see things in reference to our own short lifespan.

Anyone who visits Yellowstone should at least once use the Silvergate and US Highway 212 through Cooke City, across Beartooth Pass, and on to Red Lodge, Montana. It is one of the most spectacular drives in the Rockies.

Our route followed US 212 through Billings on to the Custer Battlefield. The battlefield and its layout are nothing like how it had been portrayed in movies. From the markers it appeared more of a running fight than a group stand. Somehow I just couldn't picture it in my mind and really couldn't get into it, but I have been there.

After spending the night in Sheridan, Wyoming, we continued east on US 14 through towns with such interesting names as Ucross, Spotted Horse, and Recluse. After Carlyle, Devils Tower grew up out of the high plains. This volcanic plug remnant was a fascinating feature. To me it is one of those things you definitely want to see, but I wouldn't necessarily go out of my way to see it several times.

So far we had pretty much stuck to well-marked US Highways, which not many folks would now consider driving, but I still do. Many sections of the old US highways have become, basically, side roads. That afternoon we began an adventure on a real gray road.

I don't remember exactly how we found it, but around Sundance, Wyoming, we left the highway behind and headed through the Black Hills.

Following a series of gravel county and forest service roads, we eventually ended up in Lead, South Dakota. Along the way, we had seen only one other vehicle, and they acted as if they actually knew where they were going. At times we straddled gullies down the center of the road and several times had to drive cattle out of way to pass them. In later years, I would drive gravel roads blocked by cattle, but I have never again found that route through the Black Hills.

My wife swears that I have never made a trip without finding at least one gravel road to drive. And come to think of it, I would be hard-pressed to name one.

We made a short stop in Deadwood, which is a place I wanted to see. After all, Wild Bill and Calamity Jane lived there. It was then pretty much a sleepy, almost abandoned town. Today, there are small casinos, entertainment, and more. From Deadwood, we made the mandatory visit to Mount Rushmore.

Mount Rushmore is a stunning sight. It is impressive in the day and awesome when lit up at night. In 2006 we visited and spent the night in a room where we could see most of it out our window. The changing lights of the sunset really set off the sculpture. Early in the morning, we visited on top of the mountain just as a thunderstorm rolled over the top. In this same visit, my teenage grandchildren got to visit with one of the surviving workers on the sculpture.

NIGHT VIEW OF MOUNT RUSHMORE
FROM OUR MOTEL ROOM

Bill and I, after staying in Rapid City, South Dakota, picked up State Route 44 east. On this route, you are just driving along through high plains prairie, then the bottom drops away. You have arrived in the Badlands National Park. Like many of nature's works, nothing, not even a picture, prepares you for the actual place. For me it was the almost instant change from prairie to massive erosion that was most impressive. The Badlands are definitely different.

Highway 44 continued to be our route across South Dakota. Even today, it remains a great way to avoid the rush of the interstate and see the countryside. I still love to drive roads through the rolling prairies on what are considered by most people the back roads. On these roads you mostly just have to watch your own driving, not the other drivers, and there are actually things to look at other than semis. . A real bonus is the small towns you pass through. Often you can find beautiful shady parks that can be a good rest stop. Most of these parks also have nice clean quiet picnic areas. However if you are not picnicking there are numerous hometown cafes with blue-plate specials. As Least Heat Moon said, "look for the ones with the most calendars and homemade pie."

Since this trip, wherever possible and practical I never drive an interstate when another road can be used to reach the same destination. On a trip to the west a few years ago we drove to St. Louis on I-64, but shortly after that drove less than fifty miles out of four thousand miles on an interstate.

After South Dakota it was pretty much just a drive home; we had already been gone a few more days than we planned. In spite of usually finding some pretty good meals, we missed Mother's home cooking. Also as usual, money was running short.

That was my first real trip west. Like the first trip with my whole family and with the grandmothers, this was my only trip ever with just my brother Bill. He went in to the Army, and I went to college (the first of five times).

I regret that not one picture survives from that trip, but many memories are etched in my mind forever. Like that first visit to the Grand Canyon, I have returned to many of these places with my wife, my children, and grandchildren, and my friends to revisit and refresh memories. Another plus for me is to see the wonder or awe that is often on the faces of people seeing something for the first. I like to refer to it as "*the look.*"

AN INTERIM

After 1959, it was eight years until I made another personal vacation-type road trip, except one with my parents. After two aborted tries at college (a great party time), I decided Uncle Sam needed me.

As a member of the Air Force, I got to see San Antonio, of course (for one afternoon). After basic training, it was off to Fort Belvoir, Virginia, to learn to fly—fly a pencil and T-square around a drafting board, that is. Washington DC was a young man's dream, with at least five young ladies for every male. You can't beat those odds! The only problem was the $52.50 per month paycheck. However, one weekend a month, it was fun.

After finishing tech school there was a goodbye trip with my parents. Uncle Sam decided that he needed me in Asia. So my dad decided they would accompany me to Travis Air Fort Base, California, before my eighteen-month overseas assignment. We flew in to Denver, rented a car, and proceeded to see Canyon Lands, Zion, Death Valley, and Yosemite over the next nine days. Along the way, we experienced a rainstorm in Death Valley and a snowstorm in Tioga Pass (in July). While we found several gray roads, the gravel road from the San Joaquin Valley over Rattlesnake Pass in to San Jose was the most memorable with an average speed of 20 mph.

ME, IN UNIFORM

ACROSS THE BIG WATERS

Getting to what would be my first permanent assignment for the USAF proved to be an adventure all its own. A contract air carrier, Riddle Air, was to supply the transport. Their DC 7 had seen better days, but that era aircraft were more comfortable than they are today, complete with good seats and a smoking lounge/bar. The first stop was to be at Hickam AFB in Hawaii after a ten-hour-flight. Somewhere just an hour east of our first destination, one of engines was feathered, but we cruised on in safely. At that point, we were told that our layover that was scheduled for a couple of hours would be delayed. Four hours later, the problem was fixed, or not. We boarded the plane and out to the end of the runway we went. When the pilot did an engine run up smoke poured from the problem engine. We headed back to the terminal and heard the announcement that it would be evening of the next day before we could resume our journey. We were taken to a motel and told that we would be brought back at six the next evening.

My seatmate, Don McBride, and I roomed together, and as it turned out, we were going to the same outfit and ended up being roommates the next eighteen months. As he was a small-town Nebraska boy, and also an early riser, we took the opportunity to explore during most of the next day. We were like two kids in a candy store, drooling over the bikinis that were not just on the beach, but seemingly everywhere.

At six in the evening, we were all aboard for another ride to the end of the runway, and a ride back to the terminal for another night island-bound. Finally, about noon the next day, we got off the ground for another nine-hour-flight to Wake Island. We had no inflight engine problems on this leg. However when the pilot revved up the engines prior to taking off for our final leg, smoke rolled from the same problem motor. Once again we headed back to the terminal. Only this time the result, rather than bikinis and beaches, was spending many hours in a hot, humid, old terminal.

Finally, we were off for another long flight to Kadena Air Base on Okinawa. Again, there were more problems this time with a small, smoking engine oil leak. We made it, landing in July to mid-ninety temperatures and 90 percent humidity. Our incoming barracks overlooked the contract carrier area, and that Riddle airplane sat there, being worked on for another two days. Looking back, it's a good thing I was young and immortal, or I might have been scared stiff for almost five days.

■

After finding out all the required immunizations had not been completed, I was required to make an extended stay at Travis Air Fort Base. Two weeks later, I was off to join up with the 1962nd communications group at Kadena Air Base in Okinawa, which would be my home for the next year and a half. . I found it interesting to live alongside another culture and to have an opportunity to explore Okinawa's coral potholes, fish in the sloughs and visit its many neat small villages. Otherwise, it was work and party.

It was after I bought a 1951 Willis (with no first gear) for one hundred dollars that the island really got explored.

As always I was able to find interesting gravel roads and interesting people. Rural people and farmers are pretty much the same everywhere, and even with a language barrier are ready to swap lies. In recent years, Okinawa has become a tourist destination for many Japanese.

During this year and one half my job was not that of a regular constructions draftsman, instead, I maintained records of cable maps, antennae farm layouts, and an occasional blowup of electronic schematics. Why? It turns out I really was not very talented or good at being a draftsman. The prime example of this was an attempt to do an overhead for the commander to give a presentation. The symbol for our communications group was an eagle on top of the world with lightning bolts surrounding the globe. Well *okay*. In reducing the big symbol, it had to be redrawn much smaller, freehand, to fit at the top of an overhead slide. In addition, I didn't have an actual overhead projector to preview my work with; I just held it up to the light and looked. It looked good to me; however, when flashed up on an eight-foot screen in the Colonel's presentation, there was this duck with lightning bolts running around the globe. Requests for further overhead illustrations ceased at that point. They let the base graphics shop handle all overheads in the future.

I wrapped up my time overseas actually a rank lower than when I went, which is a whole other story, not really appropriate here. But I had fun. My next assignment, in spite of my request for Europe, was at Andrews Air Force Base near Washington DC to a real engineering squadron. It did not take them long to discover my limitations, so I was back to power grid layouts and simple, routine task.

That is how I became the lowest ranking person in the Pentagon. To work in the Pentagon with the War Planning Division required a top-secret background investigated clearance. Having been in a high security communication outfit, I had such a clearance. And except for my section chief, I was the only one in that career field on the East Coast of the United States that had the proper clearances, and my unit could certainly spare me. Therefore, that is how this E2 airman became an important cog in the War Planning Division on special assignment to the Pentagon. In fact, I was the only enlisted person in that part of the Pentagon. Luckily, the job required something I was actually pretty good at—doing charts and graphs (no overheads). After a few months the assignment ended, and I must have done okay. The three-star general in charge called me in, told me to take a week off and go home, and if anybody asked why I was away, to just tell them to call him. I did as ordered.

I finally ended my Air Force career as an E4 (will wonders never cease) and almost re-enlisted. After four years, I had almost figured out the system and was having a good time doing some coaching and refereeing. While not a super athlete, I had become a good basketball coach. At that time, if you could play or coach, life was pretty easy in the Air Force. I think if they had approved my transfer request to Special Recreation Services I may have made a career out of the Air Force. However, I wanted to get home and resume my life as a cowboy.

MARRIED
(THE FIRST TIME)

After my four years with Uncle Sam, I returned to college for the third time. Two years later this now twenty-five-year-old decided it was time to get married. I had some of my education out of the way and managed the family farm, plus a place of my own that I had purchased.

My first wife, Mary Ann, had been on a vacation only once in her life (for a couple of days close to home) and never a road trip. She never really could understand my desire to travel and try to see it all. This, among other problems common to many marriages, finally doomed this one.

Three good things came about from that marriage and those are my three sons: Sean, Nathan, and Charles. In trying to be a good, understanding wife, she did try the traveling thing, but never quite got in to it. Mostly, she thought it was a waste of time and money. While I, on the other hand, saw it as a way to create lasting memories like my parents did for me, along with it being an important part of my sons' education as complete people.

We did have a few good trips. My dad thought every young couple should, if possible, take a once-in-a-lifetime honeymoon trip before joining the *real world*. So after our early May wedding day, we headed west for a three-week tour. Along the way, there was the Grand Canyon. One of the funniest things that happened on the trip was there. I had convinced Mary Ann that at the Canyon we should take the mule trip down.

However, at the first overlook she slowly walked over and calmly said, "Honey, I don't think I want to ride the mules down"

From there we went on to Zion Canyon and then Los Angeles, California, where my oldest brother, Charles, who was then city engineer for Arcadia, showed us the sights. After a couple of days we traveled north to Sequoia National Park to see the giant trees still surrounded by snow and back northwest to San Francisco and up the coast through fog and redwoods to Coos Bay, Oregon.

In Oregon we saw another of creation's most beautiful sights—Crater Lake still surrounded by a snow-covered rim and the ranger stations with many feet of snow on their roofs. Crater Lake is as beautiful as any place I've been—simply awesome. It is the caldera of a volcano that collapsed, leaving a nineteen hundred-foot deep lake, surrounded by the old caldera's rim. It is part of the whole string of volcanoes that stretches from Washington down in to California. This is another place that neither words nor pictures can really capture its magnificence.

From one crater it was off to see another, so we headed east on US Highway 20 to Craters of the Moon in Idaho.

US 20 was not then a crowded road, and since the interstates, has become what could almost be called a *gray road*. Craters of the Moon, along with another lava flow in Arizona, are some of the most recent lava flows in the continental United States. It lies on the fringe of the geologic hot spot that forms Yellowstone National Park.

Rexburg, Idaho, was again visited and served as a jumping off point into Yellowstone. The date was May 15, and the park had only been open a few days for the summer visitor. Roads were lined by feet of snow, and the lake was still frozen over. Again, luck was on my side. We drove in and got a room at Old Faithful Lodge for two nights with no reservations. Wonder if we could today?

One adventure while in the park involved the bears! That early in the season there were plenty of bears to be seen along the roadsides and often at stops in the park. At Yellowstone Falls we were just getting out of the car when a bear was just starting across the front bumper.

I saw his butt and said to my wife, "Get back in the car."

"Why?"

About that time, the grizzly rose up and placed his paws on the hood. No answer to that question was necessary.

BEAR ON THE HOOD OF OUR CAR

Exiting Yellowstone from the east gate, we ended up staying the night at the Buffalo Bill Cabins in Cody, Wyoming. At that time, they were very basic. In recent years they have been renovated to become what is a truly unique place to stay, a 1940s cabin with two thousand amenities.

From Cody we made a drive that I still consider one of the most scenic in the country. Traveling across the Big Horn Mountains on Alternate US 14 provides great vistas, little traffic, and a chance to chase cattle out of the road.

After the mandatory stop at Mount Rushmore, for one of the few times in my life I got frustrated and could have been called *lost*. Two hours of driving around small blacktop and gravel roads on a supposed shortcut, we could still catch glimpses of the monument. Forget the gravel shortcut that day. However, we finally got back to a main road and found a bed for the night. After the Badlands, the next day it was pretty much just a drive home. It was a memorable trip, but to this day I think that Mary Ann would have preferred a more conventional honeymoon week at somewhere nearby, not the great adventure we had.

CAMPING

After that honeymoon trip, it was almost thirty years before I took another family journey, staying in motels. Camping became the only way to go. Why? Camping could make travel affordable for me, and secondly, I really enjoy camping.

ON CAMPING

Camping comes in several varieties from the very simple to the almost obscene. Anything from a backpack, canteen, and sleeping bag to a half million-dollar motor coach has been described by their owners as camping.

Backpackers really get up close and personal with the country they walk through, getting to know it in detail. However, in talking to many backpackers, most dwell on the rigors, the physical and mental accomplishment of overcoming the hardship, as a major motivator for doing their hikes. The real plus for them is the people they meet along the way.

The other end of the spectrum was described in *Blue Highways* as "a propensity to get away from it all while hauling it along.." In other words, they have brought their king sized beds, microwaves, dishwashers, satellite TVs and an extra car. And this is all part of a fake-pine-paneled behemoth that would never survive a real *gray road.*

I guess the only way I would consider such a beast (if I could afford it) would be like a retired rancher from Alberta I met. He had sold his ranch, including his home, to a son and bought a large fifth-wheeler. The summers he spent at home helping out some on the ranch and for the winter he spent almost six months in Arizona. The RV was his home now.

That would only be an idea, because it would take the whole rig just to hold the pictures, books, keepsakes, and clothes necessary for Diane's sanity. Maybe if we both drove fifty-foot semis it would work, though.

Now I fall in to a category you might call a *tweener* when it comes to camping. I did a little (very little) backpacking in my younger days. And I had a small motor home for a while. Neither really suited me. Backpacking was just too restrictive, plus the ground is too damn hard. A motor home is not only expensive, but it is also restrictive. It seemed whenever an interesting gray road was found there would be a sign, "No vehicles over 20 feet," or something like that.

So my camping is a compromise. An extended cab four-wheel drive, F-250 diesel with a camper shell suits my needs. In addition, it can also be used to pull the cattle trailer. In it we carry a medium-sized tent, an excellent large air mattress, two oversized sleeping bags zipped together, a couple of folding chairs, two coolers, and a couple of small, stackable plastic crates (for nonperishable food and towels), plus the big black box and the puzzle box. In the black box is the Coleman lantern and stove, extra lightweight tarps and rope (for rainy times), a big pot, and stuff. The puzzle box is actually a toolbox with a carry strap and two lift-out trays. Each tray has its own purpose. The top has all the cooking utensils and silver ware, the second has matches, spices, and coffee, and the larger bottom is where the metal plates, coffee cups, and small pots are carried. If you called right now, all this could be loaded in less than ten minutes. Everything is kept in a separate place together in its container and ready to go. The freezer and pantry could be raided for enough food to last several days, in just a few minutes more.

In the summer of 2008, I was taking my youngest grandson on his first camping trip on the spur of the moment; I timed how long it took to get the camping stuff out, and it was actually less than ten minutes. Even though it had not been used for a while, it must have been put away right, because when we unpacked at the campground everything was in good shape, clean, and useable.

Now, if I can give my wife Diane an accurate weather forecast and tell her whether she will need any *dress up* clothes in case we eat out, she can be ready in less than an hour (if the decision for which shoes to take can be made). I call this a compromise, because we have some creature comforts such as our nice big air mattress and warm fluffy sleeping bag, chairs to sit in, adequate food and utensils to prepare a good meal, and a cooler full of beer (what else would I need). Yet if you choose your campground and campsite well, you can still get some of the feel that the backpacker has in the wild. And we do get away from it and not take it all with us.

We are not purist. If it turns off miserably hot or stormy and if we can't find a suitable campground, we find a motel. We are snobs about our campgrounds. If it is an RV campground, forget it, usually. If when in your tent you feel like you can reach out and touch someone, forget it. If it is in the summer with no shade, forget it. Our perfect campground is one where there is either enough underbrush or enough distance between campsites that we know others are there, but we don't feel like we are in an apartment house with no interior walls.

OUR TYPICAL CAMPSITE

We rarely find a commercial campground that meets our standards. Most are geared to the RV/travel trailer set with no real tent sites. Sleeping in a tent between two forty-foot monsters with the AC running and TV turned up is not my idea of fun. There are a few commercial campgrounds usually in the west that are acceptable.

Many state, national, and provincial parks often have pretty good tent sites and sometimes have separate areas for the tent camper. We have had good luck at National Forest, BLM, and Corp of Engineer campgrounds. An often-overlooked source of good campsites for an overnight stop on the road is city parks and even local fairgrounds, especially in the Midwest.

Camping, whether RV, backpacking, or even our compromise version, is certainly not for everyone. Whatever the method, it takes effort and some organization and planning to have a good experience. This is especially true for on the road camping with children.

FIRST-TIME CAMPERS

Our oldest son, Sean, made his first camping trip at ten months of age in February 1969. My dad had found a 1964 Volkswagen Campmobile. It was complete with an icebox, sink, really comfortable foldout bed, and hammocks hung around inside and would sleep four kids. In addition, it had a catalytic gasoline heater (never did trust that thing, but it worked). In 1968 he and my mother took it on a six-month journey across the western United States and Canada. They had never driven more than two hundred miles in one day, and expenses averaged less than twelve dollars per day for fuel, food, and camp fees.

I had quit college for the third time, so on February 1, 1969 in the borrowed camper we headed south through Tennessee and picked up the Natchez Trace. That first night we stayed in Northern Alabama along the Tennessee River at a Corp of Engineers campground. Sometime in the middle of the night, something or someone banging on the side of the camper awakened us. . When we investigated we found Sean happily playing with a fishing float dangling from a rod hanging over his bed just as other babies his age would play with the mobile over their crib. (I understand he still gets up at all hours and bangs around.)

The next day it was on down the Natchez Parkway then west. Our final goal was Big Bend National Park in Texas. After a rainy night in a Homochitto National Forest campground in Mississippi, it was on to Galveston Island State Park in Texas on the beach. All the while, I was having a ball taking in the countryside and changing landscapes. And in spite of the traveling, I think Mary Ann was enjoying the break from the daily routine as well. Except for his nightly play times, ten-month-old Sean was easier to travel with than he ever would be again.

SEAN ON THE WAY TO UVALDE

It was in Texas that I really discovered why my parents maybe had never driven more than two hundred miles in a day on their trip the year before. Flat out and slightly downhill, the big bug could reach 57 mph. Driving mostly back roads I hadn't really noticed, but in the expanses of Texas its limitations became very evident. A saving grace was the fuel mileage, which was almost 28 mpg. After driving for most of a day, I had filled up for a total of ninety-four cents for 9.4 gallons in Louisiana where a gas price war was going on.

It was cool and windy on the beach, but great for walking, and we had it all to ourselves. Traveling west across Texas, we made a visit to the Alamo and splurged for lunch on the River Walk. Staying the night in

Garner State Park a few miles west, we again had the place all to ourselves. It was a wonderful time to camp with no crowded campgrounds and near-perfect weather. After starting the mornings with a light jacket, we had warm sunny afternoons and cool enough evenings to enjoy a campfire.

The next day, in spite of a head wind that limited us to less than 50 mph, we finally reached Big Bend National Park. The desert lands have an austere beauty all their own, and at least this February it was a wonderful climate for camping with warm days and cool nights. Chisos Basin campground is near an elevation of five thousand feet and is surrounded by a rim of mountains some two thousand feet higher. The landscape seems to change minute to minute with the passing of the sun.

SEAN CAMPING AT BIG BEND

There followed three days of exploring and R&R. We took a short trip to Boquillas Canyon and rode mules across the Rio Grande (Rio Bravo), hiked some trails, and met and visited with others in the campground.

Leaving Big Bend, we headed for what became a highlight of the trip. At the camp store we saw that McDonald Observatory, located in the Davis Mountains about one hundred and fifty miles north, had a visitor viewing that night. So off it was for a stay at Davis Mountain State Park. That evening we viewed both Venus and the Moon through what was then one of the larger telescopes in the world. This was pure serendipity. Quite often over the years some of the most memorable things I've done have happened this way.

Following a visit to El Paso and Juarez, we spent our first night in ten days in a motel. We had gone north to see White Sands, New Mexico, and head east. The weather had turned much colder and, being about worn-out, we spent a motel night in Cloudcroft, New Mexico. After days of dry desert, the Sacramento Mountains were an oasis and welcome sight.

Leaving Cloudcroft, we made a side trip to visit Carlsbad Caverns, then it was flat-out at 57 mph (on the flat parts) toward home. We spent one more night alone in a city park campground somewhere and another in a motel, but fourteen days after we left, we were home.

I had left home with three hundred dollars in my pocket and had eight-five dollars left when we got home.

DISRUPTION

Often the best-laid plans end up not working out. At that point in my life, I felt that the course was pretty well set for the future. However, things change. In 1965 I purchased a good-sized farm in south central Kentucky with the plan to eventually transfer a part of the family's registered Angus herd to it. I would then have the basis to carry on a successful cattle operation for a lifetime.

Outside forces, the economy, and several circumstances brought all these plans to a halt. Many people don't remember that in the late 1960s, although interest rates were very reasonable, money was just not available to borrow. My dad's business was heavily reliant on borrowed operating money, and as he had made several major expansion moves, he was highly leveraged at that time. The bottom line was that funds to complete several big contracts just couldn't be borrowed. This resulted in the failure of his construction company. With much of my future tied to eventually taking over the cattle herd, my plans also came to a halt. I came out fairly sound financially and tried a dairy operation for a couple of years, but eventually I just sold out to regroup my life. That is how I ended up managing a several hundred-head, registered cowherd in conjunction with a small feedlot in central Nebraska.

BACK TO SCHOOL (AGAIN)

After managing a herd of cattle in central Nebraska, I was laid off during the cattle price bust of 1973. I accepted a job with an Angus herd in northern Virginia and decided to stop at home in Kentucky on the way east. While there, my dad suggested I go see a longtime friend, George Pendergrass, who managed the University of Kentucky research farms. He had been somewhat of a mentor during my teen years.

I don't know for sure, but I think some preplanning had occurred by him and my dad. During our visit, George told me that if I would come back to school he had a house and job for me. As much as I had enjoyed the cowboy life, this was home. So for the fourth time it was back to college—this time with a wife and three sons.

Looking back a couple of years ago, I figured that during that time period my inflation adjusted, disposable income was actually the highest of any time in my life. Between working, the GI Bill, a free house with utilities, and a garden, life was good. My boys still remember riding their Big Wheels around campus, playing with the students, and climbing the trees. In today's world, I would worry about their safety more, which is a sad commentary on the state of our society.

For the next three and a half years, it was classes and work. The first year and a half I worked over forty hours per week, as well as almost every weekend, plus carried eighteen to twenty-one hours a semester. It was time for a break. Loading up the 1971 Hornet station wagon and three boys, we were off. We had no real goal, except to visit an Air Force buddy in Rhode Island at some point.

You can't believe how much stuff can be packed in and on a small station wagon—tent, sleeping bags, Coleman stove, pots, pans, cooler, and clothes for five people.

We had stuff put in every hole that would hold some-thing. Leaving Lexington on August 6, we headed north-east, picking up US 62 across Ohio in to Pennsylvania, and spending our first night at Pyamtuning Reservoir in northwest Pennsylvania.

As we pulled in to camp, a light rain began to fall. The boys had already learned the first lesson on camping when it was raining; the first thing you do is put up the tent, and the last thing you do is take it down. Thankfully, we had done some weekend camping, and the boys had the drill down pat. Each one had a job to do, so in less than fifteen minutes the tent was up with sleeping bags inside, a tarp for shelter was stretched above the picnic table, and we were well on the way to preparing supper.

US 62

US 62 should definitely qualify as a gray road. Running from Buffalo, New York, to El Paso, Texas, it cuts diago-nally across the central United States through rolling hills for much of its entire length. Follow it all and you will pass through Conewamgo, New York, Tionesta, Penn-sylvania, Winesburg Ohio, Oddville, Kentucky, Cairo, Illinois, Risco, Missouri, Yellville, Arkansas, Prague, Oklahoma, Floydada, Texas, and of course my home of Lawrenceburg, Kentucky. US 62 is a great cross-section of middle America. It begins with the family dairy farms in the hills of western New York and continues through the Amish settlements of Ohio and then in to my home area, the Eden Hills of Kentucky. Slowly it turns in to flat croplands filled with corn, soybeans and rice in the Mississippi flood plain and then once again it enters hill country. This time it's the hills of the Ozarks and northeast Oklahoma. Eventually US 62 finally reaches the west someplace around Oklahoma City. There are still hills but these have longer distances between the crests. When it enters Texas it is once again in to cropland with the addition of cotton fields. Passing through the panhandle you will see the largest cattle feedlots in the world. The environment then changes to one dominated by dry. Dry mountains in New Mexico with only green in the higher elevations and finally it becomes the Chihuahua Desert before reaching the end of the route in El Paso Texas.

Few roads in the United States can offer the same diversity along its route as US 62. Carlsbad Caverns is on the route and Mammoth Cave is just a few miles south of this highway. Almost any time of year, you can find great rodeos in New Mexico, Texas, and Oklahoma. The end of the Trail of Tears is commemorated in museums at Muskogee and Tahlequah, with the Cowboy Hall of Fame in Oklahoma City, Oklahoma.

For the music lover, there is the Ozark Opera at Eureka Springs, Arkansas, where each summer budding young opera stars perform three productions under the tutelage of major artists and directors from around the world. Or Branson, Missouri, is just twenty-five miles north of the route.

In Kentucky we are proud of our outdoor musical, *The Steven Foster Story*, in Bardstown. While in the area, take in the Bourbon Trail that runs along US 62. Here at Lawrenceburg we are home to Wild Turkey and Four

Roses distilleries, both part of the trail. For the outdoorsman there are seven major lakes and numerous rivers, and canoeing the Allegheny Waterway.

If you're hungry along the route, try Paces Pizza in Jamestown, New York, (the best pizza I have ever eaten), Lamberts in Sikeston, Missouri, (home of the thrown rolls), West Kentucky mutton barbeque, and thousands of other small-town restaurants that have the cuisine to tempt you to gluttony with their blue-plate specials and homemade pies.

I have driven about all of it, but never all in a single trip. I certainly don't have the patience. If you are going somewhere and in a hurry, then forget it, but if you need a break from feeling driven by the interstate, rather than driving, it's hard to beat.

■

The next day broke with a light fog, but the rain had passed on east, and by the time we were loaded, the sun was shining brightly. Our route took us north to pick up US 20, which runs just south of Lake Eire. We travelled between fields of grapes and on into Buffalo. And you can't go to Buffalo without a visit to Niagara Falls. The falls are another of those jaw-dropping sights. Standing beside it, the sound and feel is much like standing beside a jet with after-burners on.

A few years later, while sitting at breakfast on the Canadian side, my friend, Roy Toney, (who will show up later in tales about travels with our cattle association), posed the question, "What do you think that first Indian in his canoe, coming down the river around that bend did?"

Think about that picture.

Continuing on US 20 we passed through rolling hills covered with apple orchards and fields of Holstein cows (that's the black and white ones). With the day bright and sunny, we decided to stop early. In mid-afternoon we pulled in to Sampson State Park on the east side of Seneca Lake.

Our campsite had a view of the lake where we quickly settled in, and the boys got their first real play break of the trip. As at almost every campground I have visited, one of the pluses is getting to meet your fellow campers. It is rare that you get to meet and visit with other travelers in a motel. So while the boys played, we visited and swapped stories.

That night there was a sky full of stars with a warm campfire, and the next morning we awakened to another beautiful day. We started north to the shore of Lake Ontario to explore the small towns and byways as we traveled, stopping and visiting when something interested us. We reached Selkirk Shores State Park right in the southeast corner of Lake Ontario by mid-afternoon and decided to make it another early day.

We certainly found out how cool the Great Lakes water can be even in August, but had a ball. Overnight it was windy, and the surf pounded the shore not too far from our campsite, but no rain, just a dry, late summer cold front passing by. Again we awoke to a bright sunny day

This time we did get off the less traveled roads on to I-81 north to the Thousand Islands and crossed in to Canada. Enough interstate! It was on to Ontario Route 2 and a drive along the St. Lawrence Seaway. What a sight the large ocean-going freighters were passing by. The boys just about couldn't believe it. Numerous stops were made to watch the passing parade.

At Maitland we turned north through Bishop Mills and on to Kemptville. We were armed with our trusty *Woodall's Guide,* and Rideau River Provincial Park sounded like what we were looking for—wooded and on a river. Plus, it was a short drive on to Ottawa, which we planned to visit.

This was my first visit to Ontario's Provincial Parks, and for a camper I was sold. Since that time, I have made the trek to camp in Ontario fourteen times. Overall, their parks and conservation areas are very camper friendly. Usually there is good site separation, clean shower houses, and a friendly atmosphere. In fact, one of my all-time favorite campgrounds is located just up river from Ottawa.

Settled in by early afternoon on a site right beside the river, it was off to the small river beach where the boys could swim. It was by the river that I learned about catching a Northern Pike. The young couple next to us had a canoe, and the husband went out to fish.

My middle son, Nathan, always the fisherman, yells out, "He's got one," and so he did.

I saw his pole bend, and a ten-minute fight to land it began.

All of a sudden, the fish broke water and landed in the canoe, and the man jumped out. About that time it was beginning to look like a rescue. Then he started to swim toward shore, pushing the canoe in front. As he approached the bank, I grabbed the canoe and started to pull, but almost let go. I saw what looked like two feet of sharp teeth snapping and thrashing with a vengeful eye turned my way. It turns out he had decided that he was better off with the fish in the canoe and him out. That was one big, mean Northern Pike!

During the night, the cold front had pushed well south. It was 33°F at dawn and we were not as prepared then as I am now. So the night was a real togetherness experience. I even got up in the night and put our big shade tarp over the whole bunch of us inside the tent and still it was cold.

Getting up early, I got a roaring campfire going and prepared a hot breakfast. Everyone was soon sufficiently thawed to begin a new adventure. It was off to Ottawa. Like their parks, I was impressed with the Canadian capital. Having spent over two years in Washington DC, I was impressed with the cleanliness and laidback, friendly atmosphere in Ottawa.

During that first visit it was easy to park very close to Parliament Hill and actually just walk in to most buildings. In my recent visits, tourists were standing packed in like sardines at the changing of the guard and parking was almost impossible to find. We spent the next two days walking and picnicking along the Rideau Canal, visiting the museums, and just enjoying the city. In recent years I get the impression that Ottawa has declined some. The first several visits we never saw street people, and recently some of the neighborhoods seem to have deteriorated. The atmosphere is now more like that of a large US city with the hustle and bustle. Still it is someplace I like to visit. And someday I hope to go in the winter and ice skate the Rideau Canal.

After three nights at our campground, it was time to move on. The next stop was Quebec City.

The Province of Quebec is beautiful, *but* of the six times I have been there, four times it has been a bad experience. That first visit should have been a warning.

Arriving just outside Quebec City in early afternoon, we stopped at a tourist info center. Our camping guide had provided us with a place where we would camp, just north of the city, and we were looking for some more stuff about the city. With the boys asleep, Mary Ann stayed with them while I went inside.

Going in, I just start looking around and picking up some brochures. A middle-aged man and young lady were manning the desk. While I was walking around, they were having a lively discussion about Montreal Expo's baseball—*all in English.*

After checking out the printed materials, I had a question. I can't remember what it was, but after asking *in English,* all I got was two dirty looks. Suddenly, the man burst out a string of French and walked to the back room. The young lady just continued to give me a dirty look. I left and didn't go back for over twenty years

In spite of a chilly reception at the tourist center, we found Quebec City, especially the old parts and the citadel,

La Citadelle, unique, and the flowers especially beautiful. The boys, as boys would, really got in to the fortifications and cannons. But that was enough about noon we headed back in to the United States.   Entering on US 201, it wasn't long until we made a left on to Maine Route 15 to Moosehead Lake. For the night we camped at Lily Bay State Park. The mosquitoes there were the biggest and meanest I ever encountered in almost forty years of camping. They could even leave a welt through a fairly new pair of jeans, and mosquitoes rarely give me much trouble. The only other place, almost as bad, was a campground beside rice fields in eastern Arkansas. They were as persistent, but not nearly as mean.

Just before going to sleep, the howling started from the coyotes (or red wolves) and Mary Ann wanted to know if there were bears. I usually try to tell the truth, but that night I lied. No way was I going to either load up and get on the road in the middle of the night or try to sleep five of us in that little Hornet station wagon.

Doctoring our bites, we continued on Route 15 to Bangor, then southeast to Arcadia National Park. We had hopes of pitching our tent there, but all of the campsites were taken. After a driving tour of Arcadia, we headed for US 1 and went south. That night we stayed at a very forgettable, private campground between trailers (enough said). Till this point, all the campsites had been at least semi-private and pleasant, but not this one. I sure wish I had discovered Camden Hills State Park on that trip instead of years later.

The next day we went down US 1 to north of Boston, then west to visit my older brother, Jim, who then lived near Leominster. We found a good campground at Pearl Hill State Park just a few miles north. It could have been a not so good of an experience, as sites were close and open, but we were the only ones there. And the setting on a tree-shaded hilltop was really nice. After a day's visit and another night at Pearl Hill, it was off to Rhode Island

My friend, John Hefler, and I were stationed together at Andrews Air Fort Base for the last two years of my hitch. On the surface we had very little in common other than beer drinking, but that was a start. We became life-long friends, and even when time has passed between getting together, we seem to pick up just where we left off.

John was raised on Jamestown Island in Narragansett Bay. He had been raised almost as a waterman, with much of his life revolving around the bay or a family, summer island home on Lake Winnepesaukee in New Hampshire.

JOHN'S CABIN

While in the service together, we visited both his family and mine. Afterwards, we have gotten together on an irregular basis.

At that time, he was living on Narrow River in a small place he was fixing up to re-sell. It had a large backyard that ran over three hundred feet to the river and had a large flat beside the river. This was a great place to pitch our tent. We proceeded to catch up on lots of things, including beer consumption.

Our son, Nathan the fisherman, would not be satisfied until he got to fish. (Plainly said, he bugged the crap out of us.) We dug the fishing rods out of John's garage and armed with these started to hunt for supper. In this tidal, brackish water we had no luck fishing. About all we did was lose bait to the crabs. A quick trip for chicken necks, and John's crab net resulted in a bushel full of those tasty crustaceans. Once they got past the squeals as the crabs went in to the boiling water, even the boys just about foundered for the next two nights.

The second morning it was time to head home. Gone was the time to enjoy the leisurely drives and frequent stops along the gray roads. It was hit the super slab and pedal to the metal. Classes started in four days, and funds were running low. After a night in a campground near Deep Creek Lake in western Maryland, we were back to the grind.

Although young at the time, the boys still remember this trip, not the specifics but parts. The crabs made the biggest impression. They all can still just about founder on a meal of crab, which remains one of their favorite meals.

By the way, we made this trip starting out with about two hundred and fifty dollars and had some left when we got home.

DOING THE RV THING

A year after the trip northeast, we sold a piece of property and we used that money, along with a contribution from my dad, to buy a used RV. It was twenty-six feet with all the expected amenities, on ton-Dodge chaises, and in good shape. Dad used it almost exclusively for his winters spent in Florida, so this was my first chance to use it.

A week after the spring semester, we planned to head west to Colorado. Putting the boys to bed in the camper, we saddled up and headed out about four in the morning. Running the Western Kentucky Parkway, US 60 through Missouri, then US 160 in Kansas, we spent the first night in Elk City State Park, Kansas.

Late in the night, a prairie thunderstorm roared overhead. Fortunately, we were camped on the leeward side of the dam bank, and most of the wind passed overhead. It wasn't until we were up in the morning that we heard a whole series of tornados had accompanied the storms.

SEAN, NATHAN, CHARLIE AND I AT DODGE CITY

Rolling on west, we followed US 160 to Medicine Lodge, then up to US 50, and west to Dodge City. After seeing the Long Branch Saloon and looking for Matt, Chester, and Miss Kitty, we ended up in Garden City for a night in a blah RV park.

Mid-morning the next day, the boys got their first look at the Rocky Mountains. I had never been in this way and still don't think it's quite as impressive as seeing them from a distance further north. After lunch there was a stop to take in Royal Gorge. What a sight! You have to admire the engineering and nerve of those who built it.

To this point, we had not been on a real gray road, even though US 160 almost qualified and does now. Colorado 9, then the gravel road through Guffey to Eleven Mile State Park, certainly meets the description.

Eleven Mile State Park still sticks in my mind. Set in a high intermountain basin along the South Platte River, it has a high, lonesome beauty. There is a humbling feeling of how small we really are, with the snow-capped mountains in the distance and miles of view up the valleys.

As a campground it is nothing special, but with sites set quite a ways from the others you seem to be all alone in a wild place. Short on amenities, but long on atmosphere is how I would describe it.

CAMPING AT ELEVEN MILE RESERVOIR

Leaving Eleven Mile, there was a goal in mind. There was a popular song by C. W. McCall about Wolf Creek Pass, and I wanted to drive that pass. So it was south on US 285 to rejoin US 160.

The drive on US 160 from Del Norte through South Fork and across Wolf Creek Pass was as interesting as any of the Rocky Mountain drives I have taken. Yet it is not often talked about in the travel publications. The song had it right. After you top the 10,850-foot pass, it is down, around, around, and down right into downtown Pagosa Springs. The road has been upgraded since that time. However, in early June of 1975 the high snow banks and turns so sharp you could see the rear of the RV was worth the trip. In Pagosa Springs we found a good commercial campground beside the San Juan River.

Leaving Pagosa Springs, we headed to Mesa Verde National Park. By that time we had driven almost four hundred miles on parts of US 160 in two states. For the most part it is a lonely road with long stretches, broken occasionally by small towns with grain elevators, blue-plate cafes, Conoco stations, combines on the road, and an ever increasing sense of size as you head west. In the high, dry of eastern Colorado, you can almost feel you will never see green again, but then in the distance you see the snow-capped Rockies and start to climb through evergreen forest up to snow-capped peaks.

The Mesa Verde cliff dwellings seem very primitive to live in. However, if you compare them to the rock or wood/mud huts with thatched roofs that most of our European ancestor lived in at the same time period, they actually look pretty comfortable. The villages seemed to be laid out with more forethought and planning than some of today's towns. Still, it must have been a hard existence, especially when the climate turned dry after centuries of adequate rain for maize and other staple crops. Staying the night at the park campground doesn't stir either positive or negative memories, so it must have been okay, but nothing special.

The next morning we backtracked to Durango and picked up the million-dollar highway, US 550, up the Animas River Valley with the narrow gauge railroad running parallel and clinging to the mountainsides. It takes a route climbing the narrow valley up through a ten thousand-foot plus pass. Any way you go to Silverton you have to travel through this type of terrain with narrow valleys and high mountain passes.

Silverton can best be described as interesting. It was a typical mountain mining town just starting to go touristy. Visiting eleven years later, it was still moving slowly toward development. Since I haven't gone back for several years, I guess I might not recognize it now.

ANOTHER PARADISE LOST

After that first trip to Colorado in 1959, I came away feeling that no place could be like the Colorado Rockies—winding drives with awesome overlooks and a sense of grandeur along with high lonesome and valley roads that ran through small ranching or mining towns. The towns were set in between snow-capped peaks with great expanses of the native brush, tall and short grasses, surrounding them. Rangelands had fat, sleek cows, but you wondered how they stayed so fat with what looked like sparse grazing. In the valleys were irrigated bottomlands with alfalfa growing rank and hay bales stacked by the fields. In addition, the people we met were a hardy bunch of ranchers, almost always ready for a friendly chat.

On the trip with the RV in the mid-70s, that impression still stayed with me, and I wanted to return as often as possible. For a summer vacation in the mountains, I could not imagine a better place.

Eleven years later, planning to return and visit some of the places, I discovered it almost seemed a different place. Rocky Mountain National Park and Grand Lake changed little, but the more I went, the more things had changed. The snow-capped mountains and great, wide, high valleys were still there; alfalfa grew in the bottomland and fat cows still grazed the high, dry basins.

What had changed were the towns, and even they had often encroached on the slopes. Large developments of plastic, glass, and veneer condos had sprung up like weeds in a beautiful pasture. Mountains once populated with spruce, pines, and aspen were being invaded with ski slopes, pseudo alpine lodges, and traffic. Strip malls littered the once beautiful landscape. Blue-plate cafés were hidden by poor reproductions of western cafés that served microwave prime rib and steaks.

In the campgrounds there were the behemoths with generators running and TV's blaring, and colored light strings everywhere.

I am fully cognizant that tourism can mean a better life to many rural areas and provide income for jobs lost from other enterprises. Probably in balance, it is a positive thing.

That still doesn't mean I can't feel a little loss for what was once an uncrowded, easygoing lifestyle. There was once a place that could be different—a change and not someplace set in the mountains just like your hometown. The tourists have escaped, but taken it all with them.

All is not lost. There are still those few places where the land hasn't been sold in forty-acre tracts, plastic and glass condos don't line the slopes, and there are no strip malls. You have to hunt and be willing to travel the gray roads to find them.

■

Leaving Silverton through the 11,075-foot Red Mountain Pass, Ouray, and Ridgeway, we joined US 50 at Montrose. At that time US 50 was not a four-lane road as it is now. At Grand Junction we made a drive-thru visit to Colorado National Monument. What an awesome view of the valley of what is the most important river in the Southwest. The green valley lies below and it seems you can see almost forever across the rolling high, dry basin.

Time to start heading east. We got on US 6 (I-70 hadn't been built) and reluctantly turned east. Before we reached Parachute, the skies darkened and a cold north wind started to blow. It was about three thirty in the afternoon, so we decided to spend the night at Rifle Gap State Park. It was early enough in the year that the reservoir campground had not opened yet, but the one up at the falls had opened the previous week. There were only two other hardy souls in the campground—one in a small travel trailer and two young hikers in a tent.

No sooner had we gotten leveled up, made a dash to the restroom, and returned, it started to snow. We were having a late spring snowstorm. The boys were really excited to experience what to them was snow in summer. On the other hand, I was checking the food and propane supply just in case we were snowed in. There was enough to get by for a couple of days at least. It was the first night we actually cooked and ate inside the RV on the trip.

That was about the only time in all my travels that I was glad to be in an RV with a heater, generator, and toilet. It snowed off and on all night, but the total accumulation was less than three inches. Only a small skiff survived on the road out of the park, and by the time we reached the valley there was nothing on the roads.

From Rifle we picked up Route 13 north through the ranching town of Meeker and joined US 40 at Craig. The ride up 13 still travels through the high lonesome of the intermountain basin. The landscape is one of sage, interspersed with small bunch grasses and forbs. The only trees are scrubs located along intermittent streams, washes, and Cottonwoods along waterways. Cattle thrive in what seems an extremely harsh environment. You just have to allow at least fifty acres per cow for summer grazing. The forage though sparse has a high nutrient content. A real plus is that parasites both internal and external are not a problem for cattle as they are in climates that are more humid. The cattle run on very large tracts, and they actually migrate, like the wild grazers, around the property to fresh grazing throughout the summer.

Past Steamboat Springs and across Rabbit Ears Pass it was back to a side road on Route 14. The road across Rocky Mountain National Park was not open yet for the summer, and we had planned to head north anyway to return home on a different route.

Route 14 is different from some of the other routes across the Rockies. While you do cross the 10,276-foot Cameron Pass, the mountains themselves are not as barren and bleak looking. Much of the route is through large forests of evergreens and follows small streams as it winds its way through the mountains. We spent the night at State Forest State Park amid a large grove of trees. It was a much warmer camp than the previous night, made even better by a roaring campfire.

Following the winding road down the east slope, it was back to the high plains. Turning north to Cheyenne, we decided it was time to really roll east. So with a tailwind of about 45 mph it was on I-80 east we went. At times it felt like the brake was a better choice than the accelerator. We filled the gas tank in Fort Collins and again when we reached North Platte, Nebraska. With a wind assist, we may have set a world record for gas mileage in an RV with 25.8 mpg. The night was spent at Johnson Lake Recreation Area near Lexington, Nebraska.

The next day we went to visit friends we had made while working near Genoa, Nebraska, a few years before. After spending the night at Fremont Lakes State

Recreation Area, it was an all-day drive to arrive home at ten at night the next day. Back to the real world!

The boys really don't remember much about this trip, except the snow. The places I remember most are Eleven Mile State Park and the drives through Wolf Creek Pass, as well as the million-dollar highway and the high lonesome of the great basin.

Another thing I remember is that this is the last road trip vacation that Mary Ann would ever make with us. She just didn't seem to like the traveling part of it.

Looking back, the trip to the Big Bend country and the one camping in the Northeast were the ones she seemed to enjoy.

ANOTHER INTERIM

In 1976, the year after the Colorado trip, it was time to quit being a student and go get a real job. I took a job working with the 4H program in Whitley County, Kentucky. We settled in and became a part of the community for the next five years.

While we traveled some, it was always a fast drive to a definite destination and purpose, not a journey. We made visits to Florida over Christmas to visit my father. Mother had died suddenly in early 1976, just a few weeks before they planned to make a four-month trip to Alaska.

We took the boys to play in little league football all-star games in Panama City and Fernandina Beach, Florida (and were beaten badly). And we did some weekend camping trips around the area.

One thing I did implement was a 4H cultural exchange program with 4H families in other states. Our kids would travel to visit with them, and they would return the next year for a visit with us (on the road again). We exchanged with Aitkin County, Minnesota, Brown County, Texas, and Bay County, Florida.

Most of our 4H members had never been anywhere, except for a few that had made a trip to Florida or Myrtle Beach. So loading up the borrowed school bus with tents and sleeping bags, it was off we went.

Traveling with them was quite a bit different from a vacation. Had they not been a great bunch of teens, it could have been miserable. For myself, I got to see the source of the Mississippi River and found I really enjoy working with young people one on one.

It was a success, as our teen program became one of the strongest in the state. And it was great for the 4H-ers. I have kept up on how many of those that went with us are doing, and they have become successful adults. They have had careers as Army officers, engineers, pharmacists, teachers, accountants, and business owners, and at least one followed in my footsteps as an extension agent. When I run in to them now they have never forgotten our trips and how they opened their eyes to a wider world.

LAST RV TRIP/BOYS ON THE ROAD

In the early spring of 1981, I had the opportunity to transfer in to a full time county agriculture agent position in Anderson County, Kentucky. My official date of transfer was June 15, but I took a month's accumulated vacation time and really started the new job in July.

We had unfinished business, so we decided that while Mary Ann finished up in Whitley county, I would move the boys up to Lawrenceburg just before school started. I had found a small efficiency apartment in the country to tide us over until we bought a more permanent place. In addition, I would commute back on weekends.

By then I was having road trip withdrawal. I really hadn't had the time or money to plan an extended journey. But for me, it was time. The boys had gotten old enough (nine, eleven, and thirteen) to really remember a major family trip. So I started to lay the groundwork for a three-week trip up to the Canadian Rockies, back down to Colorado, and then east home. We planned to take the now aging, but still sound small RV.

As time grew closer, Mary Ann became more reluctant to go with us. It was her opinion that we should not even consider taking a trip with an impending move for the family later in the year.

Looking back, the upcoming trip was just adding another straw to a troubled marriage. However, I was too wrapped up in career, moving, and a desire to be on the road to notice. So when she announced she didn't really want to travel, I decided to go anyway.

Since Mary Ann wasn't going, I decided to ask three of my 4H members who had been great teen leaders, gone on our exchange trips, and recently graduated from high school, to join us. They would be good company and could help drive. In addition, they had helped raise and harvest the five acres of tobacco that was providing the extra funds for the trip.

June 22, 1981 we were on the road. Leaving from Williamsburg, Kentucky, at three thirty in the morning, it was up I-75 to I-64 across to Louisville, and up I-65 to Lafayette, Indiana. At Lafayette it was time to get off interstates if we wanted to see anything, so we picked up US 52 and headed north. For the next two and a half days we would follow or parallel US 52 until we reached the Canadian border. When we found a state route running parallel, or seemed to cut across one of 52's meanders, we would take it. That first night was spent at Mississippi Palisades State Park in northwest Illinois.

Early the next morning it was on the road again through a corner of Iowa, up in to Minnesota. Shortly after passing the Twin Cities, a light rain began to fall, and speeds had to be limited. We crossed in to North Dakota at Fargo. Heading west on I-94, we ended up pulling in to the Corps of Engineers campground at Lake Ashtabula, just north of Valley City.

It was a lonely campground with only one other camper in the place, and there was a light fog for a damp night. As we got there a couple hours before dark and the white bass were running, the boys just had to wet a line. We had fish for supper that night.

ABOUT NORTH DAKOTA

Boys on the Road was my first visit in to North Dakota. Even though this time was mostly a drive through the scenery, it was interesting enough to make me want to see more. In spite of what I had heard that it was just a long boring drive across flat land that all looked the same, my impression was different. Driving up US 52 through Carrington, Ariamoose, and Voltaire to Minot was filled with long rolling hills, valleys with wheat fields that were on the way to ripening, and rocky slopes. On a hillside around most towns were signs made of white rocks honoring graduating classes, sports champions, and more. The small towns, typical of the Great Plains, each had a charm all its own. There was the inevitable Conoco station, at least one café/bar, and neat well-kept homes.

Ten years later, I had the good fortune to be able to spend a three-week study sabbatical in North Dakota. At that time, Dr. Harlan Hughes was the livestock economist with North Dakota State. Harlan was, and is, one of the very best beef herd economists in the world. After a week on campus learning about the software he had designed for analyzing herd economic performance, we spent time traveling the state visiting county agents and ranchers, utilizing the tools he had created.

The second week we visited Carrington for a state-wide lenders training one day, and for the rest of the time we did a zigzag west to Dickinson, north of I-94, then back east on a southern route. Twice more I have had the opportunity to spend time in North Dakota. Both visits involved not just a quick drive through, but also actually spending time with the ranchers and people of the state. You won't find glitz or glamour, but it is a state where you can discover less is more.

A few years later, members of our cattle association participated in a beef management school with ranchers from North Dakota, South Dakota, and Montana. In addition to classroom type work, we got to visit livestock operations around the state.

∎

Leaving Lake Ashtabula, our route was northwest, and by early afternoon we arrived at the Canadian border at Northgate. After a very thorough inspection, we were admitted to Saskatchewan. It seems the motor home in front of us was carrying several firearms and not just hunting rifles. The Canadians take their firearm rules seriously.

Proceeding on north, we spent the night at Moose Mountain Provincial Park in Saskatchewan. During the day's drive we had passed through steep hills, rolling hills covered with wheat, and finally flat prairie of almost continuous wheat fields. Very noticeable were the *fallowed fields,* which are left out of production one year to accumulate enough subsoil moisture to produce a crop the next.

From our night's stop, it was pedal to the metal west past Moose Jaw, Swift Current, and Medicine Hat—all of this right in to a strong head wind. Motor homes and head winds are just not made to work together. So after almost nine hours of driving across the hot, windy prairie, we reached Kinbrok Lake Provincial Park, Alberta. I hadn't picked up from the camping guide that the park had no showers available. After skipping that necessity the night before, I made what turned out to be a questionable decision—clean up in the lake. Even in late June it was just plain ice water. With all the chill bumps I don't think we accomplished much cleaning, but at least we washed the trail dust off.

The campground was actually kind of neat in a very open, prairie setting alongside the lake and did provide a good stop over. And we were now just a little over a half-day from our first real goal, the Canadian Rockies.

The next day it was get up early and on to Calgary. In Calgary we replenished our grocery supplies, which with six boys had been hard hit on the four-day trip west. We had just a short drive from there on to Banff, where we found a nice campsite in Banff National Park. From our site we could see several of the surrounding mountains and had a great view back to the east down a valley.

That first evening offered something I had never seen before or since. An hour or so before sunset an east wind sprang up, and what looked like a fog started up the valley. As it grew closer the perception of a greenish tint grew. When it finally reached us, we discovered that what we were seeing was a pine pollen fog moving up the valley. One other thing that had not occurred to me was the really long day light hours that far north. It was almost midnight when it finally got dark and sunrise came very early. We ended up spending three days exploring in and around Banff and up the Icefield Parkway, as well as Lake Louise and the Athabasca Glacier.

At that time you could drive right up to the Athabasca Glacier face, and it was a fairly easy walk to get up on the glacier itself. When visiting some seventeen years later, I was surprised how much the glacier had retreated, and what a hard walk it was to actually get up on it. It would be easy to say it was manmade global warming, which is a current hot topic, and yes, no doubt warming has taken place. However, when you look how far it has retreated in the past few hundred years, it has not been only a recent occurrence.

Other highlights of our stay were the sightings of moose, mountain goats, and bighorn sheep, along with a young black bear. However, maybe one of the most memorable events was bathing in the hot springs in the middle of a heavy snowfall in late June.

SASKATCHEWAN RIVER CROSSING

Up the Icefields Parkway from Banff is one of the neatest places I have ever stayed. While visiting the area again in 1998 on one to our Cattle Association Tours, we stayed at Saskatchewan River Crossing. It is located in a large valley surrounded by mountains, with at least three above ten thousand feet. There is really nothing to do, unless you are into outdoor things, and the motel falls short of a four-star rating. Rooms are fairly small but clean, and there is only one restaurant. It's not a place that the four star traveler would choose. With all that, it is one really neat place to stay. The views alone are worth the stop and stay. The rooms, lobby, and restaurant have a real authentic, rustic-comfort feel, and the food was great. I especially liked being able to grill and season my own steak. . After having a perfectly prepared steak, the opportunity to sit quietly with the sunset painting a new picture every few minutes was priceless. This was the kind of place I like to stay. It is right in the heart of a high profile area, without the pressure of having to get too dressed up or having to make dinner reservations way ahead of time; it has good food and a great view and all for a very reasonable price.

SASKATCHEWAN RIVER CROSSING

Leaving Banff about noon, we crossed over in to British Columbia with a goal to end up on the west side of Glacier National Park the next day. That night we stayed at a small roadside campground along the Columbia River. The most memorable fact about the campground was our visit just before dark by a young Grizzly bear. He just kind of made a walkthrough, and everybody just gave him plenty of room until he moved on. That did change our sleeping arrangements for the night. For most of the trip, except for the rainy night in North Dakota, the three older boys with us, along with my two older sons, slept either in a small tent or on top of the motor home on air mattresses. But not that night! We experienced togetherness that night, as well as we the next night in Glacier.

With everybody inside and very little outside to load up, it was a barely-daylight start to the day. In fact, a couple of the boys didn't wake up until we were almost back to the US border crossing at Roosville. Then we went down to pick up US 2 and travelled east to the west entrance to Glacier National Park. We had left early enough to eat lunch alongside of Lake McDonald.

After lunch we headed for the Going to the Sun Road. What a drive! It is no doubt one of the most famous drives in the mountains. It is slow and curvy with wonderful vistas around every turn. And there were still several snow banks all around that early in the year. We just took our time, stopping often in the drive to observe, throw snowballs, and enjoy.

That night found us on the east side at Rising Sun campground along St. Mary Lake. We hadn't really explored Glacier, but we had been there. And we did have another nocturnal visit from a bear. Oh well—another night of togetherness.

We got on US 89 early the next morning as we headed south toward Yellowstone National Park. This was a driving, seeing the countryside day. We passed through small towns like Dupuyer, Neihart, and Wilsall before settling in for the night alongside the Yellowstone River just south of Livingston. With campsites on a first come first serve basis in Yellowstone, we planned to be at the campground gate early enough to be sure and get a good campsite. And we were able to get a site right on the bluff overlooking Yellowstone Lake near Grant Village.

For the next couple of days we explored Yellowstone. We didn't see it all, but we tried. By the way, if you have never tried to swim in Yellowstone Lake, don't unless you are part polar bear. A return visit to Yellowstone is still on the agenda for my sons. I have been back several times, but none of them have had that opportunity

We realized the next day was the Fourth of July when I saw a flyer for a PRCA rodeo in Lander, Wyoming, and decided to head that way early the next morning. With an early start, we actually got to Lander before noon and found a really nice commercial campground just south of town on US 287. This campground was in a ranch type setting and had animals (including a butting buck), old buildings, and more, plus a good-sized stream running alongside.

That afternoon we took in the rodeo, which had some of the top rough stock riders, including Donnie Gay of world champion bull riding fame. With the long daylight hours, there was still time to tube in the stream, try for Brook Trout, and cook a good supper.

THE BUTTING BUCK

The campground was a ranch setting, and the family operating it had a menagerie of critters. This included a large Hampshire buck sheep. In fact, it was one of the largest Hampshire bucks I had seen. The boys couldn't resist taking some time to visit in the corrals, which had all these nice critters to pet. Most of them, from the chickens to the donkeys, pigs, and more, were pretty kid-friendly. This big buck sheep was too friendly and thought it was great sport to catch you not looking, get a short run, and *bang!* run right into somebody. Luckily, the first one he got was one of the older boys, and they just laughed (sheep aren't really big enough to do much to a football tackle). That just encouraged him, and pretty soon he was a constant nuisance.

I mentioned the antisocial behavior to the owner, and he said it was becoming a problem. Now just a few years before, I had been chased all over feed pens and alleys in Nebraska by a big yellow Charbray (Brahma cross) steer that had no respect for a man, a horse, or even a large John Deere tractor. The only way to get him to do anything was to let him chase you through a gate, bail out over the fence, and make sure somebody got the gate closed behind him. Besides that very afternoon, I had seen the bullfighters at the rodeo save many a bull rider after being bucked off.

So it might have been the Coors-thinking, but in my mind there was no doubt I could handle that one hundred-eighty-pound buck and teach him a lesson. Out to the corral I went, and sure enough, old buck started his assault routine. With the first pass it became apparent that it was not as easy as expected, since old buck was an experienced butter. That first pass he got a good hit on my butt (thankfully Hampshires don't have horns) as I turned to let him pass.

Okay, it was apparent that this would require more care and a solid game plan. After all, by now my three sons, three young men who I had worked with, and a few innocent bystanders had gathered to see the show. With that first pass I imagine the money was going down on buck as the favorite at this point.

However, my boys were too young to really remember that old yeller steer, but I remembered. Sometimes you just have to be smarter than a critter with a one-track mind. Now old buck wasn't as fast or the danger to life and limb that old yeller had been, so I started to play a game kind of like a Spanish bullfighter. Each time he would miss, it riled him even more.

After a few passes he was really starting to back off, take a big run, and try to knock the stuffing out of me. Then we came to the last charge. Buck having backed off about fifteen feet, he started rolling full out my way. Wait, wait, and *bang!* Buck had totally failed to see the big cottonwood tree less than a foot behind my back—just like the big yellow steer in his fury didn't see the steel angle dozer blade I had ducked under at the last second.

Reactions were the same. Legs buckled and old buck went down with a confused, faraway look in his eyes. Not really hurt, he just wandered away to the far corner of the corral. Fun time was over. The next morning old buck seemed as gentle as a lamb.

Wish I could say the same about that old yeller steer. His headlong crash in to the steel dozer blade only slowed him down for a few minutes. Two days later he caught a cowboy not looking and broke three ribs.

■

Getting a late start the next day, I had made an accounting of available finances left—it seemed, as it is all too often, that unless we headed home soon we would end up well over budget. Besides, after fifteen days everybody was starting to look forward to getting back home. So after a run down in to Colorado for a night stay in a National Forest campground near Cameron Pass, it was back to the prairie. That night in the forest beside a fast running stream that provided us with a supper of Brook trout, we spent the last night of real camping on the trip. It was one of the most pleasant, with a good campfire and lazy evening in the high country.

We proceeded on east with the goal of North Platte, Nebraska. There is a RV campground at the intersection on I-80 that had a go-cart track nearby, so it was time for the boys to have fun. At this point our trip was coming to an end.

Loading up the next day, we drove a straight run home, arriving in the wee hours of the next morning. We were tired and almost broke, but we had mostly accomplished what we set out to do—see a lot of the West.

As with many of the most memorable journeys, they seem too often to be the last. I didn't realize until writing about "Boys on the Road" that this was the last time that my three sons and I were all together on a vacation journey as boys on the road. I wouldn't trade those memories for about anything. Sure, we made trips all together to visit grandparents in Florida or go to some event, made long weekend camping trips, and two out of the three have made trips with us since, but we were never all together again on a journey.

END OF AN ERA

As was pointed out earlier the "Boys on the Road" trip just seemed to pile another brick on to a struggling marriage. Mary Ann and I seemed to grow further apart and find more differences in goals, life expectancies, and needs. Oh, we made a couple of futile efforts and continued on some, but before another year had passed, it was over. There is never a successful conclusion to a marriage, and children often suffer from their parents' inability to resolve issues, but life goes on.

So it was that I started a new life with my three sons, making a home and living our lives in a small cabin on our thirty-acre farm in the hills of Anderson County.

NEW BEGINNINGS

Many things that happen in life have a way of working out eventually. And time does have a tremendous healing effect. So for the next couple of years the boys and I existed. We tried to have as near of a normal life as possible following a family breakup, and we did the best we could.

I need to mention our little cabin was one we built out of lumber sawed off of our farm. It is made of oak lumber that we nailed up while it was still green. The foundation was laid twenty-four inches thick from field rocks that were mortared together—if not fancy, it was strong, really strong. A few months after it was built, the tractor's brake was left off and it rolled down a fifteen-foot hill in to the backside of our cabin. The only damage was a loud thud and one stud was moved about a quarter inch.

While it did have electricity, the only water was what I hauled from town, and the bathroom was a washtub and a path. A wood stove provided heat. In very cold weather I would sleep in a chair (with no blanket) set back from the stove, so if during the night the fire died down I would get cold, wake up, and stoke up the fire.

During this time, the only traveling we did or could afford was a visit with my dad in Florida over Christmas in 1983. Finances were tight, and going from two incomes to one necessitated lots of cutting corners.

I don't know how well the boys remember how we survived during that time, but I remember doing anything to add a dollar or two to our budget. What I remember most was getting up at daylight and cutting cedar trees down for an hour or so, and then heading to work. In the afternoon I would trim the limbs while the boys hooked them to the tractor, and we pulled them out of the woods. Then at least one day during the week and each Saturday we would load the cut-up logs and deliver them to the mill. We cut over a thousand trees over the next few months.

One thing the boys do remember was the month of pork chops. While shopping one day there was a real deal on overstocked pork chops—nearly a hundred pounds at thirty-nine cents a pound. So into the freezer they went. For the next month it was pork chops grilled, baked, fried, stuffed, stewed, stir-fried, cacciatore, and various other ways. To this day they like to tease me about this, and it's a wonder they will even look at a pork chop.

TWO YEARS LATER

In very late 1983, I had been a single dad for almost two years, and while we got along, it was about time for me to start socializing with the opposite sex again.

Not really being in to the bar scene and not knowing how to start a new social life in the adult world again, I got lucky. There was an article in the paper about an organization designed for single parents, the Parents without Partners group. I decided to attend one of their meetings.

I don't know how it operates across the country or even now in the Central Kentucky area, but at that time locally it was a strong, active support group. The first meeting I attended was an educational session conducted by a family life specialist from the University of Kentucky, who I had done some work with in my job and knew he put on really good, meaningful programs. I came away impressed; their policy was that they equally balanced educational, social, and family programs.

It proved to be a good support group and a gentle reintroduction to the adult social world, and the boys enjoyed the family outings. The second event I attended was a Christmas social complete with a DJ and dance floor. I have always enjoyed dancing, but had memories of rejection as a young man when I asked a girl to dance. That didn't last long. Sitting there minding my own business, nursing a beer, and enjoying listening to music was short lived. Less than ten minutes passed until one of the members came over and said I had sat too long, and it was time to dance, so I did. It was great for a damaged ego!

Enjoyment quickly overcame my lack of courage, and maybe I didn't, but I claim to have danced with every lady there before the night was over.

I did not ever really date anyone during this time, but I thoroughly enjoyed new friends and re-entry into the adult social world. It was a different time from the 60s to the 80s.

THINGS CHANGE

A few months later it happened. At one of the parents without partners meetings, there was this very nice lady who was there for the first time. Diane sat beside me during the program, and we struck up a conversation. She had two daughters near the ages of my boys, was a teacher, and had been divorced a little longer than I had. We seemed to enjoy each other's company and conversation. Later we joined others that went to a lounge for some dancing and late evening libation. We danced for the first time, and I definitely was attracted. She now says it was my dancing and the smell of wood smoke on my clothes that really attracted her.

We left it at that and went our separate ways, meeting a couple more times at a PWP meeting and social event. I finally got up the nerve to ask her on a real date. She replied that before she would date, there were a couple of things to take care of. *Okay,* nice brush off, especially when she wasn't at the next function and hadn't called as she said she might; I figured it was just time to move on.

Well, thank goodness for our messed-up phone. While not on a party line, my neighbors and our phone both rang for incoming calls. She had called twice and never could get a hold of me. The second time she left a message with my neighbor's teenage son for me to call her. Almost unbelievably, he passed the message on a couple days later, and I did call. The rest is history.

So we started working toward a more serious relationship. We went out, did things together, and let our kids get to know each other. Fortunately, they got along great.

By late summer, we knew we wanted to be in a permanent married relationship. So instead of asking her father, we asked our kids.

Their reply: "What took you so long?"

So Labor Day weekend of 1984 Diane and I had a small wedding with just our kids and were married by a friend of mine who was the county judge.

We became the Cantrill bunch. Want an adventure? Try getting married with five teenagers. But no Alice came with the deal. For years it almost seemed as if all we did was wave at each other as we passed on the road to cross country, band, track, clubs, etc. Our budget often looked like the national debt with four proms in one year and four teenage drivers.

We talk now and wonder how we survived building an expanded cabin with family slave labor and great neighbors who helped out a lot. But we did. It took almost a year to get our current house built, not finished but livable. After over twenty years, I am still upgrading and renovating. Maybe if I ever feel satisfied we can start another one.

A really great bonus to all this is that I found out that I had also found a soul mate when it came to traveling, looking for the off the beaten path places, and finding beauty in what to many people may seem ordinary. She had never camped and never been on my type of road trip. But she has taken to it like a duck to water.

So after a quarter of a century, when I say let's go, all she asks is, "What clothes do I need to take?" (And I better be specific or the truck is full—always be prepared.)

SIDE TRIPS

Before I get in to our first *big* trip this would be a good place to mention some of what I call a side trip. The first one we made together was to Florida to visit with my dad over Christmas. It was old hat for the boys and me, but for Diane it was the first trip to the sunshine state. Like my grandmothers, she had a great tour guide. I was determined not to make it only a pedal-to-the-metal, sucking-diesel-fumes-on-I-75 trip.

We did drive parts of that interstate, but as much as possible took the older routes. We had a picnic lunch just south of Cohutta, Georgia, at the trout hatchery. After lunch we made it through Atlanta on I 75 and then got back to side roads. We passed through Griffin, Roberta, Perry, Abbeville and Ocilla. By the time we reached Valdosta it was time to find a place to spend the night. The next day we rejoined US129 in Florida and followed it to the junction with US 27, which we followed all the way down to my dad's place at Sebring. Some of the beautiful, sparsely populated, pure southern towns were still on this route at that time.

In a trip this past summer, I took the old roads down and the interstate back. Guess what, there was less than two hours difference in drive time, and I got about three more miles per gallon.

From 1949 until the early 1980s there probably were at least sixty trips to Florida. Between my dad expanding his business in to south Georgia, having several good bull customers in Florida, and going to my parents place, first near Fort Meyers and then over in the center of the state, it seemed that travel to Florida was just routine.

From 1953 until 1968 I had spent every Christmas, except while in the Air Force, in the Fort Meyers area. There wasn't a greater place to be.

I wanted to take my new wife to some of my old stomping grounds on that visit in 1984. Between new roads, subdivisions, and strip malls I was lost. Even worse, the pristine Sanibel Island was being overrun by condos and developments. The meandering Estero River that ended in San Carlos Bay amid mangroves and oyster bars was being invaded by development.

Many a day had been spent slowly motoring down that narrow river just to stop at an oyster bar while waiting for the high tide, and break off a few for a snack. Then out to the small passes and flats for redfish, sea trout, or parking over a grouper hole. A lot of it has become dredged waterways and filled mangroves swamps.

I understand the need for economic development, jobs, tourist dollars, making a living, and people wanting to enjoy the wonderful weather, but I don't have to like what it has done to what were once pristine wilderness areas.

This past summer I took my grandson, Austin, back to his home near Clearwater and again made the trip down on the older routes. There were pockets of changes, and development was evident along the way, but it was not obscene.

That is until we got down into Florida, north of Clearwater. Miles and miles of trailer parks, subdivisions, and strip malls had sprung up since my last visit a few years before.

Even over in the center of the state, citrus groves are filling with the same type of development.

But all is not lost. A little later in this story will be some places I have found in Florida that still retain some of the old-time flavor I remember.

VISITING THE IN-LAWS

Another side trip, or in this case *trips*, were the visits to see the in-laws. When we got married, Diane's parents were a fairly short drive up to visit in West Virginia. But shortly after, her father decided to hang it up, after being a mine equipment salesman for almost fifty years, and they moved to the small town of Poquoson, Virginia, that is on the Chesapeake Bay just south of Williamsburg. Diane's sister was there, and the climate was definitely milder than in the mountains where they lived.

So it became at least a once or twice a year journey due east to see the in-laws. We could leave our house, get on I-64, and not have a stoplight from our home until a half a block from their home. Not very often was this how it went. In looking at the maps, I remember at least five different ways we have gone. That is not counting breaks off of I-64 for some relief from the diesel fumes.

A couple of times it was a strategy to avoid bad weather in the mountains. Other times it was just that we wanted to see something different. There are some beautiful drives through rolling hills and neat farms all across Virginia.

If not in a hurry, I liked dropping south through Cumberland Gap across on US 58 to pick up I-81 near Kingsport, then up to Roanoke. From Roanoke we would get on

US 460 through Appomattox and Blackstone to Petersburg where we would head over to Virginia Route 10 and down to the Scotland Ferry. The Scotland Ferry goes across the James River to Jamestown. From there we could take the Colonial Parkway that ended close to our destination.

It was on a first trip that way when roads were snow-covered in West Virginia that we discovered the Surrey Inn. Arriving early for the ferry schedule, we had passed the restaurant a couple of miles back, and it was about lunchtime. It proved to be a good place to eat. Some of my favorites are their peanut soup and homemade pies (gluttony, anyone?). Since that first time, we have stopped back for lunch and even come back across the ferry for a nice drive, ferry ride, and lunch with the in-laws.

This route adds some miles and time, but is a pleasant ride. If we went hell-bent for leather, it was about ten hours on the interstate—if there were no construction, wrecks, or traffic jams in Charleston or Richmond—and a day to recover.

Most times our trips were during spring or fall breaks. Getting everything ready and the cows all set for our absence often meant not getting away until late morning or early afternoon. So a good stopping point for us was at White Sulfur Springs (nope not at the Greenbrier), which let us roll in to Poquoson about noon. We did discover kind of a neat place for breakfast. I can't remember the name, and the food was good but nothing special, but there was a model train running up high on the walls in the restaurant. All of us kids really liked that.

Scheduling so that we would get to the in-laws about noon was both a problem and an opportunity. Now you have to understand that my mother-in-law was the daughter of a railroad conductor, and Dot was a person that had to have a schedule. It was her schedule, and we knew better than disrupt it.

As my father in law would say, "Damn'it, Dot, the train doesn't always have to operate on your schedule," but it did.

Well, the second time to visit we arrived in the area about ten thirty in the morning, and she wasn't expecting us until after one. So we went exploring and ended up driving to see the Yorktown Battlefield. While wandering around the small town, we spied a restaurant at the end of the street along the waterfront. There we found almost heaven in their crab cakes and clam chowder (not a feature in Kentucky). I may have eaten better, but can't remember where, so it became a goal to be too early and have lunch at the Yorktown Pub.

Over the years, we found several other good places to eat in that area, but the Pub remained our favorite place. While on the visits, my father-in-law and I often escaped and explored the area. In addition, after a couple of years there he became friends and breakfast buddies with several of the watermen on the Chesapeake Bay. This was how I came to find sources of fresh bay oysters and live crabs that took up space on the way home and was followed by a neighborhood feast.

One of the most talked about trips to that area was the first time we took our two oldest grandchildren along (ages five and two). Everything went smoothly, until the second day. They had had enough of listening to the talk and watching out for great grandmama's stuff with no place to play. In other words, both became the terrible twos!

So Grandpapa had the bright idea to take them to the city park to play. No more than a block or so toward the park with Raffi singing "Baby Beluga," they both passed out. For the next two hours, I cruised and they slept. But whenever an attempt was made to change the tape to a more adult style of music, they woke and whined. Therefore, I heard "Baby Beluga" at least twenty times. Finally, we did make it to the park, and they became almost normal again for a while. However, for the next few years when anybody wanted to know the words to "Baby Beluga," I could do it and tell them how to find their way around Poquoson, Virginia.

Stories that are considered side trips are being included to make a point. Most of us have places we regularly need to go. Some are not too far, and others are a full day or so away. But any routine trip can become a gray roads adventure that adds to memories and is a step toward seeing it all. Adding a back road, a little longer route or stop somewhere you have seen but never bothered to stop, rarely adds much to your travel time. All you need is a willingness to get off the beaten path, even if just for a while, and try something new. So many of the places we remember came from serendipity.

OUR FIRST BIG
TRIP TOGETHER

By the summer of 1986 we had been in the new house almost a year. And other than the two side trips, we had pretty much kept our nose to the grindstone with work, the farm, and kids with always too much on the schedule.

The national county agents' meeting was to be held in Colorado Springs in late July. I had several days of accumulated vacation time available, and Diane was on summer break, so we decided to make it an extended trip in the west. I was allotted eight days of travel and meeting time, then planned to take extra vacation days between two weekends. So we had several days to work with.

Asking the kids who wanted to go for a camping trip to the west, we could come up with only two volunteers. Our oldest daughter, Mindy, was on break after her first year in college. Our oldest son, Sean, had just graduated high school and was preparing for college, so he decided to stay home and look after the cows (and party). Fifteen-year-old Missy really didn't want any part of it. That left fifteen-year-old Nathan and thirteen-year-old Charles as the only ones to go with us.

So we started to get ready for seventeen days of camping. As always, Diane's first question was, "What clothes do I need?"

And as always I said, "Not too much. Just some camping clothes, one nice outfit for the banquet at the meeting, and, oh yes, be sure to have your long johns packed too."

At that point she was sure I was certifiably nuts. It was ninety-five degrees that day.

All loaded up, we had the boys sleep in the back of the truck to make it easier to get an early start. Well before daylight I was out on to I-64 rolling west. Nathan didn't wake up until our first real stop at the arch in St. Louis. We got there while McDonalds was still serving breakfast. After a visit to the arch and taking in the Remington western art on exhibit, it was wagons-ho west again.

All right, I had had enough interstate. A few miles west we got on to Missouri Route 19 up to 22 and west through Mexico, Missouri, to pick up US 63 north to hit US 36 west. We had not pre-planned any particular place to stop or camp, but our atlas showed we could reach Pershing State Park by around four. It was a good time to stop.

Pershing State Park has a nice wooded campground and a small lake with a beach for swimming. Well, the boys knew the routine from earlier camping trips. Get unpacked, get set up, and then do what you want. Diane could hardly believe that about fifteen minutes after arriving we were ready to sit back in the shade and pop a top on a cold one while the boys headed to the lake. Later we started to get ready for supper—I'm a pretty good camp cook. By the way, I do most of the day-to-day cooking at home. Diane broke her right hand (the only one she can actually use) in a car accident just days after we were married, and there was a definite culture shock trying to cook for three teenage boys. At that point, her first camping experience was going really well, until . . .

Shortly after supper in the lingering twilight came the invasion of *the coon*. He was a pushy, big old raccoon, well versed in camp mooching. Straight to the trashcan one of the boys forgot to put the lid on he went. What followed could have been straight out of a Lucille Ball show. Nathan went over to harass him some, and he waddled off a little way. The top was now on. Never fear, it took only seconds for him to pop the top off and begin digging again.

All the while, city girl Diane had lots of tough questions. Would he bother us, get in our tent, or bite, etc? Then came the showstopper. While the coon was deep in the can, Nathan quietly slipped over and slammed the top shut, and Charlie quickly put a forty-pound rock on the top. You have never heard such squalling, scratching and racket. Even folks way across the campground could hear it. About ten minutes later the furor was still going on.

Okay, let's turn him loose. Carefully and quickly, we took both the rock and top off, preparing to defend ourselves from his revenge. Out he came, and as fast as he could he ran across to the far side of the camp and into the woods, never slowing down. I don't know if he ever came back that night, but do think that wise old raccoon figured it was not worth the chance to be harassed by teenage boys again.

We survived our first crisis and the greenhorn camper reassured us that all was well. Then, right before bedtime at dark, Diane headed over for a last pit stop at the shower house before turning in for the night. I'm sitting there enjoying a cool quiet night by a dying campfire when *crash!*

It turns out that another woman had driven over for a last nightly visit. Instead of putting on the brake, she had pushed the accelerator, jumped the rock curb, and crashed in to the L-shaped entry to the rest room. Guess who was sitting on the throne at that time?

Things did finally calm down, and our nerves settled. This was quite a way to start our first night of camping!

The next morning after a leisurely start, we wandered our way to Lincoln, Nebraska, where we stopped at the planetarium at the University of Nebraska-Lincoln for a break and picnic lunch. That afternoon we did get back on the interstate for a run to stay at North Platte, Nebraska, for the night.

Diane had never seen a rodeo, and at that time there was the nightly rodeo just north of town. We ended up staying at the commercial campground that we had stayed in during the "Boys on the Road" trip.

Naturally, the boys would rather ride the go-carts next door than take in the rodeo. Therefore, we were able to both escape the kids for a while, and Diane could see her first rodeo. She has since become a big Professional Bull Riders fan.

That evening while at the rodeo, Diane also got to experience her first prairie thunderstorm. It was not really big, but it was impressive for a first timer. The tent did not blow away, and the boys did have enough sense to get out of the storm. In fact, Nathan got lucky by meeting a girl whose family was on their way home to Colorado Springs. They corresponded some for a few years, and he later saw her again while in the Army in Colorado.

At least the passing storm cooled things off from the mid-90s temperature and made for a good sleeping night.

Rolling out early, we picked up US 30 and used that route to follow the north side of the Platte River to Sterling, Colorado, and then west on Colorado Route 14.

THE DRUNK LADY WITH THE BIG CAT

I can never think about Sterling, Colorado, without recalling an incident near there about a dozen years ago.

My middle son, Nathan, had always liked the west and was then living in North Platte, Nebraska, where his first son was born. A few months went by and I really had no opportunity to get out to see the new grandson. With North Platte being about halfway between Omaha/Lincoln and Denver, I started watching for deals on a flight. I finally did find a special into Denver for a little under one hundred dollars in early November.

I would leave early on Thursday morning and be able to drive back to North Platte by mid-afternoon. That part worked out great. I even ended up taking a bump for a free flight and somehow got to Denver a few minutes earlier than originally scheduled.

However, being independently poor, I also searched and found a great price on a rental car from the *worn out car rental* company. It was less than half the price of a regular company, well it should have been. The car ended up being a five-year-old Chevy Citation with 135,000 miles. My first mistake! Second mistake—I decided to take the bring-it-back-empty option.

The visit turned out well, and the grandson is turning out to be a great kid. It was time to head home. I wanted to see some cattle a little northwest of North Platte, so I headed out late morning to make an afternoon visit up near Whitman. From there I would drop back down to Ogallala and pick up I-80, then I-76 back to spend the night near the airport for an early morning flight.

All was going well and on schedule as I hit the Colorado border about an hour before dark. Looking at the fuel gauge, it still read a third of the tank and should have been good to about Fort Morgan where I could stop to eat and get enough fuel to coast in to the airport. Mistake number three.

About three miles before the Sterling exit, cough, cough, *die!* The tank still showed about a quarter. Wrong. Now it was twilight. In addition, there were no cell phones at that time.

Nothing seemed to be on the road, except eighteen-wheelers doing 80 mph in the left lane. Minutes (that seemed like hours) passed by, and it was growing colder and darker all the time.

I knew the rest area could not be much over a mile up the road, as the lights were starting to be visible in the distance. Therefore, as it was getting darker I decided to walk for help. Well, did you know at the edge of the shoulder on I-76 there are deep drains? I found one quick enough. I decided that what I did not need was to be away from the car in the cold and dark with a broken leg or worse. It was head back to the car wondering how cold it really would get and how long the flashers would continue working.

Five minutes later, a savior! A two-year-old Lincoln Town Car does a 180-power slide across the median and roars up beside my dead vehicle.

Interior lights turned on, I see an apparently nicely dressed, good-looking, early forties woman who ask, "Need some help?"

Quickly, I gave an affirmative reply.

Well, she said, "Hop in and I will take you up to town."

Okay sounds fine.

By then the window was all the way down and I could now see the entire interior and smell it as well. The fumes alone could have given me a buzz. To top it all off, perched on the rider's seat was the biggest damn cat I have ever seen. Well, maybe it would be okay, and it was getting darker and a lot colder.

Then she said as I was starting to get in, "We can just go back to my place, have a drink, and get your car later on."

Nope, maybe in my misspent youth, but not this fifty plus, happily married man who had just seen her do a power slide across the median.

I said then, "Maybe I just better stay with the car; you just call the service truck when you get back to town."

Gravel flying, off she went.

Luckily, two minutes later a nice couple stopped and said they would go by the rest area and have someone come to my rescue.

The story didn't quite end there. No more than five minutes later I saw the Lincoln making another power slide across the median. Once again there was a request to just hop in and she would take care of me.

"Just get in and we can go on to town."

Guess she might have felt rejected, but I did reassure her help was on the way.

Sure enough, a roll back showed up a few minutes later, took me to town, and filled the tank.

As I related the story, the operator just laughed, "We know who you mean. "Every time she starts drinking she cruises the interstate and rest area looking for a night's companion."

Not many can tell about being solicited by a good-looking drunk woman with a big cat in the middle of nowhere.

And I have never used the take-it-back-empty option again

■

Colorado 14 was the route that I wanted for Diane to first experience the Rocky Mountains slowly grow out of the horizon. At first it is a cloud that slowly grows as a recognizable, large chain of mountains. Diane had grown up in the mountains of West Virginia, but had never experienced the grandeur of mountains over twice as tall growing out of the prairie. Needless to say, that became a memorable ride.

Our first night in the Rockies was spent at Aspenglen National Forest campground near the entrance to Rocky Mountain National Park. It was okay, but not anything to write home about. Thankfully, it was not a cold night, as there were some small forest fires in the area, and campfires were banned. With a Coleman stove supper, it was our first night in the big mountains.

In the morning it was off to explore the park. Things change over time. The guest ranch my brother and I had stayed at years before was closed and was now only an open mountain meadow. The biggest change for me was that the trail we rode up on horseback was now a one-way gravel road up to the top of Fall River Pass. It was still awesome, but not quite the same thrill as doing it on horseback.

Once on top at 11,796 feet, the boys wanted to finish the climb to a summit near the visitor center. So off they jogged, quickly at first, then gradually slower. However, they were in good shape and made the top still at a jog. I, the heavy smoking, fat man, managed to walk around some without passing out.

After exploring some more, we traveled down to the west and set up in Timber Creek campground where we enjoyed the cool mountain air and adjusted some more to the altitude. At mid-afternoon we explored Grand Lake before returning to a peaceful setting with a campfire to sit by.

It is a good thing that I am an experienced fire builder, as that night Diane's long johns were put to use. By morning it reached twenty-six degrees. We were, as they say, snug as a bug in a rug with our minus twenty degree rated, double sleeping bag.

By the time Diane was up, there was a roaring fire and coffee ready to drive away the chill as the sun came up over the mountains. However, the boys were a different story. It almost took a stick of dynamite to blast them out of the tent. They finally appeared still in their sleeping bags and half hopped, half crawled to the back seat of the truck. It was that morning we discovered the Lone Moose Café in Kremling. Turning south on Route 9, we followed the route I had traveled before.

This was when it first hit me how much it had changed. Development had encroached on the hillsides and small towns. Condominiums, ski slopes, strip malls, and pseudo western cafes seemed to be intermingled with fast food and convenience stores. Actually, the ski slopes rather reminded me of the changes brought about by strip mining in Appalachia.

Reaching Hartzel after a side trip on gravel roads to Eleven Mile State Park, it was on to Colorado Springs. We had arranged to stay at a commercial campground out Colorado Avenue on the west side of the city. For an in-town campground it was not too bad. Sites were decent-sized, and there was a designated tent camper's area. For the boys there was a pool and lots to do. In addition, Diane had a big shade tree to sit under, chill out, and read a good book while I was at the meetings.

On Sunday there was a big family barbecue picnic with buffalo and entertainment, which kicked off the national meeting. For the next couple of days I attended the meetings, learning sessions, and actually received an award for the Livestock Development education programs I had been doing in my county.

By Wednesday, with the meetings scheduled to end that evening, we decided to start the rest of our journey. Heading south on Route 115, we picked up US 50 at Penrose, then headed west. After a photo op at Royal Gorge, it was on to the west. I was hunting—hunting for a place away from the plastic, glass, strip malls, and condominiums—hunting for a place to experience the mountains off the beaten path as I had on other previous trips. And I did!

Just past Gunnison, we took Route 149 south. I found a campground listed that was nine miles west of Lake City on Cinnamon Pass Road. Well, why not try it? As we headed south, the countryside became more of the high lonesome that I remembered from a quarter century before.

As we turned off Route 149, there it was, my gravel road alongside a mountain stream. Nine miles later at around nine thousand feet elevation, we reached Castle Lakes Campground. There we settled into one of their tent sites overlooking a small lake and surrounded with enough underbrush to screen us away from other campers.

What else could we want? There were several mountains topping twelve thousand feet in view, a small Aspen grove-covered slope behind us, a beautiful small lake complete with a busy beaver family, and humming birds that were plentiful enough to sound like a bee swarm.

For the next three nights we really relaxed, hiking during the day, swapping stories with fellow campers, and thoroughly enjoying ourselves, and of course, Nathan was fishing in the lake.

During our stay we drove up toward Cinnamon Pass past a big cirque and got a closer view of the 14,034-foot Red Cloud Peak. Looking at a forest service map, I noticed that the road did run across Cinnamon Pass down through Animas and into Silverton. We wanted to visit Silverton, so this route could save us over one hundred miles.

Asking around, we were told that usually nobody tried that route, except in a jeep or smaller four-wheel drive pickup. There is nothing like a challenge! Tell me it would be hard to do, and that was enough. Besides, it probably would not be much worse than my driveway, just longer.

Off we went early in the morning to conquer Cinnamon Pass. I was wrong, but the locals were as well. The road was rougher and narrower than I expected, but even in my two-wheel drive super cab, there were not any problems. All it took was care and patience.

Often there were large rocks embedded in the road that could only be passed by running one side up and then easing over. Several of the turns, with the long wheel base truck, required going part way around, back up until the rear bumper was hanging over the cliff, and then complete the turn. A short wheel base jeep would have been a lot easier, but we made it.

At one point Nathan, who was back in the camper shell, woke up and looked out the back into almost one thousand feet of nothing. He quickly crawled through the rear window and settled in with us. I am just glad Diane learned to drive in mountains with drop offs, sharp curves, and switchbacks, so it did not really bother her too much—well, maybe just the one time when she looked in the side mirror and saw a big drop off just a few feet from our rear wheels as I backed up.

Finally, after twelve miles in an hour of twists, turns, and constant climbing, we reached a wide flat with a sign that read, "Cinnamon Pass, Elevation 12,684 Feet." We had made it! Now we could stop and relax with time to look at views that were awesome, to say the least.

In the pass at the top, a large mob of sheep in the thousands was grazing the slopes all around, while being guarded by a shepherd on his horse. He had a rifle at the ready in case of predators. While stopped at the top, we also got to see the only Martin (a wolverine-like critter) that I have ever seen.

Heading down the western side proved to be much easier than our ascent. After a few turns and switchbacks, it became a pretty fair gravel road the rest of the way.

That was a true gray-road adventure for us. I have the tee shirt that says so, even though there wasn't any place to buy one there. Although it has been over twenty years and we have been to lots of other places, this still ranks as an ultimate gray road.

When we got back home, a big thunderstorm had really washed-out our driveway, so it was every bit as rough as Cinnamon Pass, just shorter. So I wasn't all that wrong after all. Somehow, it just hasn't worked out to go back again, even though I swore to repeat it. Oh well, just another place added to the list to see again.

Silverton had not changed much in the decade since I last visited. It still retained that rough and ready mining town atmosphere, even though it had become more tourist-oriented. From there we went south on US 550 to Durango, then west to Mesa Verde National Park.

We settled in to the campground in early afternoon and proceeded to take in the cliff dwellings and visitor center. The boys didn't really remember our earlier visit, being so young at the time, but they do now. This was another first for Diane. Like before, the campground must not have been either really good or bad, as I have no recollection of it, just that we stayed there.

Early the next morning we again picked up US 160 through the Four Corners area for a photo op, where the four state marker is. It was during this morning we experienced our second rain on the trip. Summer thunderstorms in the great basin are an altogether different experience. Years before on the trip with my parents, we had a storm while in Death Valley. Even though not a big rain by eastern standards, I still remember the gullies and arroyos filling so quickly with a torrent of floodwaters.

This one was short lived, and we soon passed out of the rain shadow. We hit US 191 north and zigzagged northwest on various roads. Along the way we hit the edge of Monument Valley, Natural Bridge, and stopped for lunch where we crossed Glen Canyon. The thermometer said 108 as we found shade beneath a large, slanted rock alongside the road. At that point I did a hurry-them-up act.

I casually asked, "Wonder if there are any sidewinder rattlers back farther under the rock?"

Lunch was finished really fast and not just because of the heat.

On we went through Capital Reef National Park with the heat making it too miserable for much more than photo ops along the way. At Torrey we turned south on Route 12 with the goal of camping at Bryce Canyon National Park that night. Route 12 is often listed among the top scenic drives in the United States.

My parents and I had stayed at the lodge at Bryce Canyon in the early 1960s, and the canyon was just as I remembered it. It is uniquely different from any place that I have visited. We pulled in to the campground with lots of daylight left. After a quick supper, it was off to see the sunset.

Sunsets are one of our favorite times. Over the years, we have tried to capture pictures of them from east to west and north to south. In reality, while we have hundreds of pictures, only a few actually come close to grasping the moment.

Sunsets in the canyon country are not like anywhere else. Not only do you have the expanse of a changing sky, but also the ever-changing hues of color down in the canyons. Bryce is one of the best at this. It's almost like being surrounded by the sunset, rather than observing it in the distance—another one of those moments.

Diane and I got up early the next morning to see the sun rise up over and finally down into the canyon. It was maybe not as impressive as the sunset, but it was awesome, never the less.

Following a leisurely breakfast and load up, it was off to see another canyon, the Grand Canyon. We arrived in the early afternoon on the north rim and pitched our tent in what is a really good national park campground. Not big on privacy, the sites were nevertheless well spaced out, clean, and had a mix of sun and shade. Plus, each morning there was a big group of mule deer with trophy racks that wandered the campground grazing. It was about all I could do to keep deer slayer, Nathan, from trying to figure some way to get one for his bedroom wall.

I have talked about the Grand Canyon before, and every return visit hasn't diminished the almost awestruck feeling as I get that first good look. This was my first visit to the north rim, and I actually prefer it to the south rim. I think this is because it is less crowded and has a more laid back atmosphere.

After spending all the next day exploring and hiking around the canyon, it was time to start heading east. On the drive into Grand Canyon, a grinding clicking noise started up in the right front wheel. We needed to get some brake work done. Our original intention was to cut across to Canyon De Chelly, then on gray roads wander across to Taos, New Mexico. However, with the brake problems we decided to cut across to Window Rock down to Gallup and pick up I-40 to Albuquerque. We hoped to get a brake job before reaching there, but no luck. It was an interesting drive through the high desert—pine breaks that are interspersed with dry pasture and runs past the three mesas.

I only wish that I had been a Tony Hillerman fan at the time and not had brake problems. It would have been great just to poke around the area and drive more of the roads and places he describes so well in his mystery novels. Maybe someday.

A few years later on one of the cattle tours, I had the opportunity to spend time with a Navajo rancher in that area. He wasn't much of a Hillerman fan, but both his wife and son were. They thought that the books did give a pretty good insight in to some of the culture.

We made it to Gallup shortly after noon, stopping for lunch at a great little Mexican café. To this day, I have never eaten as good of a Chile Relleno as I did there. When I visited a few years later, the place was no longer there. A fast-food restaurant is now at that location.

A short run that afternoon put us in Albuquerque where we found a repair shop, but some parts needed to be ordered that wouldn't be in until the next afternoon. So to a motel we went, our first on the trip. Luckily, we found a motel located on what was old Route 66. It was in the Spanish style and had been recently renovated. This turned out to be a really good place to stay a couple of nights, and the boys had TV again.

With the brake drag getting increasingly noisy, we didn't do too much exploring, but we did get to see some of the city. The boys, by sleeping in, missed a great breakfast burrito the next morning, but this was another first for Diane. I have been back to New Mexico a few times and think it must be the salsa capitol of the world. Never have I ordered a meal that didn't come with a side of salsa.

After two nights in civilization, it was back on the road again. There were two more places we wanted to visit, Santa Fe and Taos. Santa Fe is an interesting blend of the old and new, but even then it had lost some of the unique flavor I experienced years before on a cross-country trek.

Taos was just starting to show the effects of the invasion from the outside and on its way to becoming an artist and yuppie community. I really liked it and would consider it a place to spend some retirement time, but from all I read it has become too expensive and too developed for my taste.

After another night in a campground in the hills east of Taos, all good things must come to an end. It was time to get back east and to the world of work. With the camping gear packed away, it was just a drive home. We traveled east on US 64 to spend the night at Alva, Oklahoma, then took US 60 to Mountain Grove, Missouri, and finally across Kentucky to home.

Seventeen days after we left, we arrived back home. Everything was going good there. The only thing was every steak in the freezer was gone, and there was a trash can full of empty beer bottles and cans. I still wonder what all I missed.

This was the first of many camping adventures that Diane and I have shared over the last quarter of a century. As with many of my memories, it was also a last. This proved to be the last journey that our son, Nathan, made with us. After this trip he finished school, went into the Army and then in to the world of work.

While it may seem that I haven't said too much about our youngest son, Charles, that's because there are a couple of very special trips we took with him a few years later.

CANADIAN YEARS

For a couple of years we traveled mostly on short jaunts in the surrounding states for short camping trips. Too often campgrounds we found were mostly suited for motor homes or trailers or were too rustic. We just couldn't find our kind of campground.

Remembering the great camping trip I had made to Canada over a decade earlier, I suggested we head that way. With Diane teaching, any extended trip we took had to be in the summer. We are not hot weather campers, so there was a good chance to find a little cooler weather in Canada.

In 1989 we made our first camping trip to Canada and fell in love with the clean small towns, neat farm-steads, and roadside produce markets, and, for us, great campgrounds. For the next fifteen years there were only two summers we didn't make a visit and camp with our neighbor to the north.

Many of the trips have a tendency to run together in my mind, but with the help of Diane's logbook and pictures I can piece together quite a bit. In the first years it was just Diane and I, but in later times there were travels with Charley and then with our oldest grandchildren.

The other thing we have done is to use different routes through Ontario and even Quebec to add to the diversity of visits with my friends, John and Ellen Hefler, in Rhode Island and my brother, Jim, in Massachusetts and to visit New England states.

People have often asked me, "Why go to Canada?"

I guess that between that first trip years before and the first trip Diane and I made, we found ourselves comfortable and relaxed on our travels in that country. As I indicated, their parks and conservation areas usually have our kind of campsites. The weather has been good for camping 90 percent of the time, and for much of this period we hit a favorable exchange rate that stretched our finances.

Most of our camping has been in Ontario, but we have made journeys to Quebec, New Brunswick, and Nova Scotia.

OUR FIRST CANADIAN TRIP

In early July of 1989 we loaded up the now aging F-150 super cab that we had taken on our trip to Colorado and the Canyon lands before. Luckily, we had a couple of the kids still home to look after things while we were gone.

With our new, smaller dome tent, sleeping bags, air mattress, and other assorted camping equipment, we headed out early on a Saturday morning. We were not nearly as organized then as we are now. The black box and puzzle box had not yet evolved. They were actually the brainchild of our son Charles.

There are several ways we have headed up in to Canada. The most frequent route has been up I-75 or most often parallel to it, crossing over at Detroit to Windsor. Like our trips to Virginia, we could leave home and not hit a stoplight until just before crossing the border if we wanted to.

Most of my friends and neighbors, when I talk about heading to Canada, always think of a long trip. However, when I tell them that I can be at the border before they can get to Atlanta on their way to Florida, they almost don't believe me. From our house on an early weekend morning without too many construction delays it is less than six hours.

This first trip we used I-75 to north of Dayton, then up some side roads to pick it up again north of Lima. There was quite a lot of construction on the interstate in the area we bypassed. We still had a picnic lunch on the shores of Lake Erie in Michigan.

Crossing the border, we went east on the 401 to Tilbury, then got off on to Route 2. After a couple of stops at roadside markets and a stop at the beer store to get some Blue, we settled in to our campsite at a conservation area near Wardsville.

Conservation areas are to my mind very much like a hybrid of our Corps of Engineers and Soil Conservation Districts. My experience has been with their campgrounds and day use areas, but not with their full function. The campgrounds are usually fairly well laid out with decent facilities that are clean and safe. Only a couple of times have I stayed or visited at one that I wouldn't go back to again.

We stayed at the conservation area near Wardsville a few times, but I think it no longer has overnight camping. At that time a local farmer whose place joined the park oversaw the campground. We had a nice visit after supper to swap lies and compare notes on farming.

Diane's notes say it was well shaded and quiet, and we had it almost to ourselves. Another of her comments was about the mosquito population. They weren't too bad but you stayed aware they were around. Maybe it's because I am a smoker, mosquitoes really don't bother me too much, but they just love Diane.

For this entire trip the weather was great for summer camping. We had almost-hot days and cool nights where the sleeping bag felt good by morning.

The next three days we just wandered east and north. Along the way, we visited London, which I had enjoyed on my first trip to Canada as a teenager when I attended a cattle sale at Prospect Farm. After that it was mostly side roads up through Stratford, Fergus, Elora Gorge, and Orangeville to end up staying near Alliston at another conservation area.

At Alliston we visited a farm roadside market that I had visited on a cattle association trip in 1985. They had great fruit and vegetables, along with homemade breads.

From there we made a swing south of Lake Simcoe, then back northeast to spend a night at Sharbot Lake Provincial Park. It was not the best park campground we have stayed in, but it was okay. We now had a goal to visit Ottawa.

In checking with the parks in the area, it seemed only a park upriver from Ottawa had any number of campsites available. So to Fitzroy Provincial Park we headed. This was to prove one of our all-time favorite places to camp. That first year we were not able to get a choice campsite, but it was still really nice.

Since that time we have been back several times, and with reservations we can get a great campsite. Fitzroy Provincial Park sits on the Ottawa River and has the small Carp River running through it as well. The Ottawa is good to canoe, and the Carp is a pretty good tubing stream. Plus, there is a decent beach, even if the water is a little cool for a southern boy.

In all recent visits we have had a campsite there that backs up to the Carp River where there is a small waterfall. The falls are just the right size to sit below and let the water roll over your neck and shoulders. With a Blue in hand it just doesn't get much better than that. As with most of their sites, you know you have neighbors, but there is enough screening brush to still have privacy.

We ended up staying at Fitzroy for three nights. During the day we explored Ottawa up river on the Quebec side, stopped at a local county fair, and rode a ferry back across to Ontario, then had time for some canoeing and the beach.

One of the places we visited was the town of Arnprior. We ended up liking the town with the Madawaska River running through it that has some neat shops, a small farmers market, and friendly people. I can't remember if it was this year or another, and Diane's notes don't say, but we noticed flyers for a benefit concert to be held there that night. Featured performers were Garth Brooks and Shania Twain, all for ten dollars each. We didn't go. I sure wish that opportunity would come around again.

Well-rested and refreshed, it was time to head for home. Up early, it was south to cross back in to the United States and pick up I-81 South to 90, and then west. By late afternoon, we reached Geneva State Park along Lake Eire in Ohio. No gray roads that day.

The next day it was back to the side roads down through Ohio. Like I-75 on our way up, there was a lot of construction on I-71 at that time.

We arrived home with plenty of light left and well satisfied with our first trip to Canada. The house was even better with Missy to keep tabs; there were still steaks in the freezer and no trash cans full of beer cans. But we still wonder what we really missed.

The next few years we made several variations of this trip, staying at different parks and conservation areas and definitely taking different routes while traveling.

SHOWER ADVENTURES

In 1991 we decided to take a route through Canada on our way to Maine and to visit with my brother just west of Boston. What I remember most are two of Diane's shower adventures.

Leaving early, we entered Canada through Sarnia and proceeded to Lake Callistoga Conservation Area near Listowel. It was typical of the conservation area campgrounds, and this one had pay showers.

Diane headed for the shower, while I was getting supper ready. A while later I was beginning to wonder what was taking so long. Looking up toward the shower house, I saw a toweled head poking out the door and a hand waving vigorously. It seems that after the first quarter and getting lathered up, the second quarter wouldn't work. And she didn't have another one with her.

Well, another quarter didn't work either. So it was, with no other females around, I had the privilege of taking buckets of water to douse her clean of soap. Diane is a little hesitant about public showers, but not so much now as then. Okay, just a blip and she wrote it off as an inconvenience.

However, two nights later back in New York camping at Cranberry Lake, bad luck hit again. We had arrived fairly late and put showers off until the morning. Loaded up except for clothes for the day, we would shower and head on east. That night at Cranberry Lake was the coolest camping we had since Colorado. Into the shower she went, and just as I am getting ready to get in the shower, there was a bloodcurdling scream from the women's shower. You got it—-Diane. Because of the previous experience, she was determined not to get caught soapy if the shower quit again. She lathered up and then turned on the shower. The only problem was that the water was *ice cold,* and she took the full force. The water heater had broken down during the night!

It's just a good thing her earlier camping experiences were good, or I think our camping days would have come to an abrupt halt.

NEW DISCOVERIES

When traveling, we do like to revisit places we have enjoyed or found interesting, but at the same time keep looking for something new. Whether it is a really great gray road, a town, a campground, a hotel, or a restaurant makes no difference. If it is something we like, we make a note for future reference.

The same trip as the shower adventures we ended up making several new discoveries. Even if they are well known we like to think we made new discoveries on our own. After leaving Cranberry Lake, we headed on over to Vermont and then to New Hampshire. Again using our trusty *Woodall's*, we found Moose Brook State Park near Gorham, New Hampshire.

Nestled in a wooded area near Mount Washington it has a good campground and a great stream fed swimming pool. Most of the sites are nice and some are really good. But what set it apart in my mind are the people who I have met that operate the park. In the several times I have returned, they have offered great customer service.

Even better is that we got lucky on our timing. It was during the Fourth of July celebration time, so heading down in to Gorham, New Hampshire, we were able to experience the local fair, concert, and fireworks show. It's a great place to have an American experience.

The second place we hit the next night. Going on to the coast, we even considered not camping at all but staying in a motel instead. Finally, on a whim, we checked with Camden Hills State Park in Maine and they had a space, so we tried it. It was not the best campsites and a little open, but acceptable. The trip up Mount Battle, along with the views is priceless. In addition, the town of Camden is really kind of neat, even if it is a little touristy for my taste. We did have grilled lobster at our camp that night. We discovered Maine ferries out to the islands as a cheap, interesting way to visit and enjoy the small islands that dot the coast of Maine.

The third place we discovered on a later trip. Again, around Fourth of July week we left Gorham, heading to visit my friend John in Rhode Island. Well, I made the mistake of going over to the coastal route, thinking we would head south, stay in a motel, and head to John's the next day. There's nothing like thousands of lobster-colored beach goers and miles of traffic jams.

While at lunch, I saw a flyer for a place called Cape Ann Resort in Gloucester, Massachusetts. So I decided to call, even though I doubted we could get rooms that night. Well, they had just had a cancellation. We took it.

Cape Ann proved to be a delight. It was not fancy but set right on the marina, and it had a free sunset cruise on the Anasquam, a good restaurant, and whale watching—all for not too high of a price.

When we inquired and found out that there was room on the next morning's whale watch trip we just had to go. After sighting twenty-one whales, mostly Humpbacks, the next morning, we were sold. We have since gone whale watching on both coasts and back again to Cape Ann.

In recent years, we have returned several times to stay at the Cape Ann Resort. It has become one of our favorite side trips. We especially like to go for our anniversary weekend, which falls on Labor Day. The city of Gloucester usually has a Navy cruiser visit that you can go out to tour; there is a boat light parade at night and fireworks over the harbor. And the crowds are not too bad for all that is going on.

ANOTHER SIDE TRIP

Until I started a new job at Keeneland Race Track, during the race meets after retiring, we usually made a short trip during Diane's spring break. Sometimes it was just a long weekend in Nashville, Smoky Mountains; other times it was most of the week.

During spring break in 1993, we decided to go and camp in the panhandle of Florida. I had visited there a few years before and camped at St. Andrews State Park near Panama City. Usually during the spring break period, weather is pretty nice in that area for camping and beach walking, which we both enjoy.

Picking up Diane after her school day on Friday, we headed south on I-65 with a goal of getting to a motel near Birmingham by bedtime. Between the rain and thousands of cars loaded with people headed the same way, we only reached Decatur, Alabama, by nine in the evening. So we found a place to stay to wait for the rain and let the crowded highway ease up some.

Rolling out before daylight, we headed on south on some roads that were not as crowded. We reached Panama City Beach in early afternoon after a great lunch at Page's Barbeque in Bonifay, Florida.

What a change it was as we rolled along at 5 mph through crowds of teens. I knew it had become more popular for spring break, but never imagined it quite like this. At St. Andrews it was the same.

"Sorry, campground full."

But the camp ranger there did have a suggestion. He would call over to the campground at St. Joseph Peninsula State Park fifty miles east to see if they had room. They did and would hold a site for us.

Things really *do* often work out for the best. It was a great place to camp. The sites were a little small, but most have good screening undergrowth, along with a family atmosphere. Best of all, it was just a short walk through the dunes to a beautiful beach.

OUR FIRST VIEW OF THE BEACH AT CAPE SAN BLAS

What amazed us most was the wide white sand beach, and much of the time you could only see a handful of people around. Each day dolphins cruised by almost on schedule. If you wanted to really get away and were ambitious, there is a several-mile hike around the point of Cape San Blas. Getting the idea that we really liked it?

The only drawback was the high IQ raccoon. The whole time we were there it was a battle of wits. He could open the cooler, pop a top on the beer, steal the ham, and leave the bread on a sandwich. Worse yet, when he got caught at it he would head up the tree to sit and look down with a s***-eating grin on his face. The only two nice fish I caught he managed to steal while I was over at the restroom for a very short pit stop.

The next day, we headed out to get some supplies and buy some seafood. The day before we came through Port

St. Joe. At that time it was a town with an abandoned oil refinery and had the great odor of a wood pulp factory. Since then it has done a great job of developing the old refinery, area and the pulp plant has controlled the smell. It's a really nice town now.

So instead of back to Port St. Joe, we headed to Apalachicola. Early in this story, I said that some places in Florida still had the look, feel, and charm I remembered from my younger days in south Florida. Not a fancy plastic and concrete town, Apalachicola still retains the small-town friendliness and ambience of an old Florida city. And there are just a couple of stoplights.

In addition, there is a good supply of bay oysters and seafood at reasonable prices, and some pretty good restaurants. We have made several spring break trips back to stay in the Apalachicola area.

In 1994 Diane and I didn't make the mistake of going through Panama City, but just went straight to stay on Cape San Blas at the state park. The next year we were joined by our son, Charles, and in 1997 by our granddaughter, Ashley, and 1998 joined by her brother, Taylor.

ASHLEY FISHING WITH GPAPA

Then after Y2K we rented a beach house with various combinations of our children and grandchildren for a couple of years, all at Cape San Blas.

On our last trip down in 2005 Apalachicola had seen a few changes. Yes, some development is taking place, but not the almost obscene proliferation of plastic and concrete seen many places in Florida and Port St. Joe has done a great job of maintaining that old-time Florida flavor.

This is a place we have considered as a real potential spot to spend some time during late winter, if we ever really hang it up. The weather is not as warm as farther south, but very few days reach as low as freezing, and there is that outstanding ambience for us.

NORTH UNTIL WE GET COOLED OFF

The summer of 1993 we had a really hot July. Diane was teaching summer school that ended on July 30 with the school year scheduled to start again the 11th of August.

We both needed a break and a getaway. So the travel plan was to head north until we got cooled off or ran out of road.

At ten in the morning I picked up Diane at school where she was finishing up paperwork, and we headed north. There were no gray roads that day, just pedal to the metal north. We were driving her new Dakota extended cab, but had no camper shell.

We reached the Big Bend Conservation Areas near Wardsville, Ontario, well before dark. It was still warm but some better. At lunch the next day in Elora Gorge, we shared a picnic table with a nice Canadian couple about our age. It turns out she was a teacher also. So while the teachers swapped war stories, I shared American blend cigarettes and lies with the husband.

We travelled on north on side roads, staying the night at Nottawasaga Conservation Area near Angus. From there we followed the eastern side of the Georgian Bay up toward Sudbury.

One of the things Diane wrote about in her log was the changing landscapes. We were getting up in to the Canadian Shield. There were lots of small lakes, granite boulders, and bogs, but no moose were sighted in them. Around Sudbury the landscape where they have mined is austere and wild looking.

After dodging a bear on the road, we settled in to our campsite at Windy Lake Provincial Park north of Sudbury. We were almost by ourselves with just a handful of other campers and had a great campsite. It was cooler, but I still didn't have to put on a jacket yet. We visited this campground again when we were headed west from Fitzroy Provincial Park to take the ferry across the Georgian Bay to the Bruce Peninsula.

During the night, there were a series of almost-severe storms. We stayed dry, and Diane didn't freak out too much. But by morning it was clearing and cooler.

On north we went, even passing a sign that said we were crossing the continental divide where the steams flowed to the Arctic Ocean. Stopping for gas about mid-morning, I noticed a local map on the wall. It showed a logging road heading west that eventually passed Chapleau and Shoals Provincial Park.

With the day much less humid, we decided to try going that way. After what seemed a lot of miles of sometimes gravel, sometimes dirt, all the while dodging log trucks, we reached Chapleau. I had found a real gray road this time.

Shortly after, we pulled into the Shoals Provincial Park and settled into our campsite. Beautiful, our site sat about fifteen feet above the small glacial lake and had an unobstructed view of both the lake and sky.

As the loons gave their eerie call, I had to put on my jacket and stoke up the campfire. Shortly after, we got to witness the almost-full moon rising up through the pines and over the lake.

MOONRISE OVER A CANADIAN LAKE

The next morning we stopped in Wawa at Young's Store for a brunch. I don't remember the breakfast, but do remember the stuffed moose.

For years Diane wanted to see a real moose. And until 2006 in the Bighorn Mountains, this stuffed moose was the closest she came. We spent a lot of time in moose country but had just missed them, I guess.

After Wawa we just wandered along the shore of Lake Superior, taking in the waterfalls and magnificent views along the way. Diane managed to add probably fifty pounds to her rock collection. She has collected rocks on every trip we have taken and has them in her classroom. Her science students always really like to look, feel, and ask about them. That night we stayed at Pancake Bay Provincial Park on the shores of Lake Superior.

We had much too short of a trip, but it had finally cooled off for a day or so. It was back to the United States where we picked up Michigan State Route 66 from the north, almost all the way to the Indiana border. We spent our last night of camping at Pokagon State Park in Indiana. Back to the work world.

DOWN EAST

In 1994 we took what was to be one of our longest camping trips. We were headed to Nova Scotia. About noon on July 19 we headed north in the Dakota pickup with a goal to camp the first night in Canada. Normally it is pretty easy to do, but not this day. After fighting traffic backups, construction, and just plain miserable driving, we managed to make Sterling State Park in southern Michigan.

It is a long drive to the east coast of Nova Scotia and that had not been a great start. However, rolling out really early, we kind of made up for it the next day and reached Sharbot Provincial Park about six thirty in the evening. It was a long day, but a lot of ground was covered. We usually try to limit driving time each day to four to five hours and stop by mid-afternoon, but we had a goal.

The next day, according to Diane's log, we had breakfast, showered, packed, and were on the road by 7:20 the next morning. We made an obligatory stop in Ottawa at Byward Market, saw the changing of the guard, and had lunch.

Crossing the river into Quebec, our plans were for us to spend the night in a commercial campground in the Trois-Rivieries area. The afternoon was turning extremely hot and sticky, and by late afternoon thunderstorms were starting to pop up all around. We decided that since it was so hot and there were several thunderstorms around, it would be a great time to be civilized for a night in a motel. So we found the Hotel Normandie on the north side of Quebec City.

This wasn't actually the second time to be in the province, as we had used it to cross on east and back down in to the United States, but never stopped. But it is the second time I had actually planned to do something besides drive through as quickly as possible.

This time after a great pizza, several bottles of Blue, and a good night's sleep, all was well. Again, we rolled out early and then headed to the old town. We got there early enough that the only places open were where all the working people were having breakfast before they started their day. There's nothing like a blue collar working man's place for a good breakfast.

Even after breakfast, practically nothing was stirring. We walked some of the streets, peering in to the shops and watching the day start. It was a cool, slightly foggy, drizzly morning great for walking.

After the street walking, it was on to the citadel and park areas above the river—beautiful in the early fog as it began lifting into the now sunny morning. It was a time we enjoyed and wanted to come back. Okay, now Quebec is batting five hundred in my book.

Leaving Quebec City, we went up the south side of the St. Lawrence, past all the dairy farms with fields of oats and peas and pastures with good looking Holstein cows. At Riviere De Loup we crossed southeast into New Brunswick.

Following the Saint Johns River, we ended up camping in Mactaquac Provincial Park just west of Fredricton. All in all, this was a great day with easy driving and wonderful scenery along the way. Tomorrow we would reach one of our goals.

For years we had heard of the Bay of Fundy, home of some of the highest tides in the world. We were to discover that, like so many places we have visited, no picture or movie could really capture the awesome feeling of experiencing the place. Nothing in our past experience prepared us for the four story high tides. It is almost unbelievable to walk on the ocean floor and just a couple of hours later see it covered with almost fifty feet of water. Boats in the harbors rest on wooden cradles when the tide is out.

We arrived at Fundy National Park before noon. The morning had been almost hot, but as soon as we pulled in to the Wolf Point Campground there was a definite climate change. With the forty-five degree bay just below and a nice ocean breeze, it was almost jacket weather. While camping there, any time we went inland it was almost hot, but pulling back in to our campsite was like walking in to a cooler. Great!

All set up, it was time to explore. Our first jaunt was along Route 915 to visit the lighthouse at Cape Enrage. What a great view of the mud marsh, walking on the rocky beach and seeing Nova Scotia just a few kilometers across the bay.

The collection of rocks began there. Diane loves geology and rocks, so she will collect as many rocks as she can convince me to carry. Then it was on to the Rocks Provincial Park to see the Flower Pots (shown below). These massive rocks stand up from the ocean floor, eroded and weathered over eons of time. Walk down the staircase from the bluff and you are on the ocean floor. When the siren sounds you better head back to the steps, as a forty-eight foot tide means business when it starts to roll in. We tried to wait for the full tidal bore, but light was beginning to fade.

DIANE AND THE FLOWER POTS

The only drawback to the Wolf Point Campground was that no campfires were allowed. With the cool nights, fog, and ocean breeze, a fire would have felt good. Diane's notes did praise the beauty of the setting and the quality of the showers.

That evening, after getting shut out at the lobster market, it was canned LaChoy for supper. But after supper we had a great conversation with our neighboring campers.

They were teachers at a boarding school just north of Montreal. The wife taught literature, and the husband was the winter sports instructor. His opinion of Quebec officials was not much higher than mine after the first visit years before. Suffice it to say, he was not French Canadian, but from Scotland. They camped in the Maritime Provinces each summer and provided a lot of local information and things to see.

The next day started so foggy that it was like a light drizzle. I was to find out that whenever the breeze was from the southeast, the day started that way but generally cleared by mid-morning. With what we thought was to be a dreary day, we decided to drive down to Saint Johns.

We wanted to see the reversing waterfall, which is where it is a waterfall in low tide, but when the tide rises enough to become a flood up the river, it appears to run backward. While on the overlook, which was also part of a tidal generating station, Diane did it. Leaning out, bracing herself against the building to get a better picture, she triggered an alarm. With a bewildered look and red face, she was quickly surrounded by officialdom. At that point I at least tried to look concerned and not laugh. She is still ticked off that she didn't get the picture she wanted.

After a great Lobster salad lunch at Don Cherry's in Market Square, we followed a gray road along the bay to

St. Martin, which was a quaint, interesting village. Mid-afternoon it was time to head back to camp. Before we did, we walked a rock spit out toward the bay, and guess what? Collected more rocks.

Looking at the map, it appeared to me that there was a gray (gravel) road shortcut across to the park, rather than go all the way back around to the main road. After the first couple of miles, it was very much like the logging road we had driven in northern Ontario the year before. To this day, Diane insists I was lost. However, I still maintain that only a wrong turn was made.

Another thing Diane noted in her log was that I got frustrated. She was right. I did—a little bit because of a missed turn, but mostly because she kept getting more and more worried that we were lost forever in the woods of New Brunswick and let me know it several times. I even got to the point that, even as a man, I would have asked for directions. The only problem was we never passed a farmstead or house or even another car. All's well that ends well—not too much later we pulled back on to the blacktop about five miles before the Fundy Park entrance. I think that proves I wasn't lost, I just didn't know exactly where I was.

In today's GPS era she would have been more at ease. However, for me, using a GPS generated route often tries to send you back to a main road, whereas my goal is to ride an unmarked gravel road. Plus, for me, it sometimes takes the sense of exploring and the unsuspecting adventure out of just searching your own way around.

After another day of exploring (and rock gathering) the weather was a little warmer, even in the evening. Late that night there was rain, and it looked like it would be a dreary day. So getting up and loaded early, we headed for our next goal, Nova Scotia.

Along the way we got to see the tidal bore travel up the river near Moncton. According to a local we talked to, it runs so strong sometimes you can surf up the river. We had hoped to cross the ferry to Prince Edward (there was no bridge at that time), but there was almost a day wait if we did.

The route we ended up taking was along the bay that separates New Brunswick and Prince Edward. Along the way we passed through the town of Toney River. We just had to stop for a photo op, as Toney is the name of my cattle association, traveling buddy, Roy Toney. I wanted him to know he was famous, even that far north.

Looking back, we wish that we had continued on to Cape Briton, but you can't always see everything. So that left both Prince Edward and Cape Briton for another time. We settled in that evening in Boylston Provincial Park that is located on a high bluff overlooking Chedacbucto Bay. It had one of the most beautiful views of any camp that we've ever stayed.

It was a lonely campground—just us and a handful of others in a pretty good-sized campground. As the sun started to drop below the mountains to the west, the fog started to roll in from the sea. By dark it was so thick that lights would only shine a few feet in front of us, and walking out to the bluff we were lost in a world of clouds.

Cooking supper was a wet adventure without a rain. Snuggling into our sleeping bag, it was off to dreamland.

In the morning with everything about soaked from the fog, we made a quick stop for showers at the golf course in Guysborough and were off on a bright, sunny day. Having no camper shell on the truck made life a little harder in damp weather. The rest of the morning and early afternoon were spent wandering on a sunny day along the coast. The drive along the Atlantic coast twists along with the small bays and inlets through small, picturesque fishing villages. While in some ways reminiscent of coastal Maine, it has a lot wilder feel and certainly doesn't have the touristy development.

Our lunch was fresh mussels direct from a mussel farm along the coast. Great eating! During the afternoon we picked up fresh, Atlantic salmon to grill that evening. One of the great things on this trip was that we almost relived the spring food chain. In Ontario we had fresh sweet corn and cherries. Quebec had strawberries coming on, and then we had fresh seafood in the Atlantic Provinces. On every trip we try to always stop for whatever local product is in season.

The plan was to have an early camp along the coast or just inland at Kejimkujik National Park. Alas, every time we tried to stop, everything was full. But serendipity often works wonders. We ended up a little later in the day than we wanted to at a small campground in Valley View Provincial Park near Bridgetown.

The views were as impressive as the night before. The park is located on what we would call a hogback around here, which is a narrow ridge. It sat several hundred feet above the valley, and the Bay of Fundy was just to the west. Grilled salmon with Nova Scotia's own cold Alexander Kent, along with a great sunset, made for one of the places I most remember camping.

After a beautiful clear, cool night it must have been time to get up early. The air mattress slowly started hissing just before daylight, and we don't sleep well on a bed of rocks. With the sun peaking up over the valley and a cup of coffee, we decided to drop down in to Annapolis Royal to find a laundry mat, do clothes, and have breakfast. Good thing we did load up, since before we reached town it started to rain.

Annapolis Royal is really a neat town. I just wish we had more time to explore some. But with homemade blueberry muffins and clean clothes we were off to catch the ferry at Digby. After getting our ferry tickets, there was time to do some exploring and souvenir buying.

Nothing in my past experience prepared me for the ferry. We had ridden several ferries, but not one almost the size of an ocean liner. What seemed almost a mile of cars, campers, buses, and semis all fit into that ship—all aboard for the three-hour ride to St. John New Brunswick.

The ship's food included probably the best fish chowder we have ever eaten. Shortly after getting underway, the fog started to close in again. With my belly full of warm chowder and the fog nestled about us, it was time for me to take a nap. So climbing on the padded life preserver chest, I had a great snooze.

I know Diane could have used a nap to, but would never do that in public. I, however, after years of sleeping in the cattle barns at state fairs, didn't care who might see me stretched out getting some Z's. I woke up as the fog cleared, and we headed in to the harbor at St. Johns.

That night we really got to experience the extent of the tides in Bay of Fundy. We stopped just short of the US border at Oak Bay Provincial Park. The park is set near the end of Passamaquoday Bay. Our campsite sat right on the shoreline.

As we set up the tent and prepared supper, the ocean lapped just feet from us and was still just starting down as we headed into dreamland. Imagine my surprise when just at dawn I got up to build up the campfire and make coffee with no ocean in sight. I could see almost a half-mile across the mud flats with no water anywhere.

Crossing back in to the United States, a great adventure was essentially over. After an overnight visit with my brother Jim in Massachusetts, we headed west. Our last night was spent in Jamestown, New York, and a celebration at a favorite pizza place, Paces Pizza. Then we went home to tell of all we saw and the memories we built. On this trip we both often experienced that feeling, and I am sure we had the look of wonder in our eyes on many occasions. And, oh yes, we had managed to keep the total weight of the rocks to under one hundred pounds and didn't have to pay duty on them.

ANOTHER SIDE TRIP

During the 90s a place we enjoyed visiting a couple of times was San Antonio, Texas. For our anniversary over Labor Day we sometimes would take an extended weekend trip. This time we flew out on Thursday evening and came back Monday. With lots of preplanning and shopping, I managed to get great deals on airfares. Twice I was able to secure a companion pass so that the total fare for two was about one hundred and fifty dollars. These low fares are rare now, but I still manage to get lucky sometimes.

My key to finding good deals on airfares is to start early and be persistent. Usually I will start at least six months ahead, use fare trackers, and watch for specials. It is not unusual to find a deal that is available for only a couple of hours. If I don't find what I consider a great deal, we just don't go. How and exactly why airfares do what they do is anybody's guess. Even an acquaintance, who was a hub manager for a major airline, told me he could never figure it out either.

Earlier in a couple of the stories I mentioned visiting San Antonio. As with almost all cities, I don't care to spend extended time there but do enjoy visiting. This first time Diane and I visited we arrived just before ten in the evening, since we left after her school day. We checked in to the Crockett Hotel, which overlooks the Alamo, and proceeded for a nightcap on the River Walk.

The River Walk in San Antonio is a place designed for the tourist trade like I usually avoid. However, for some strange reason, I truly enjoy it in not too big of a dose. One of the neatest things we did on this trip was to attend a Flamenco festival at one of the stages they have along the river. There seems to be music almost anywhere you go.

Another attraction of San Antonio is the good selection of Tex-Mex food. It may not be the best, but we are partial to Mitiara, which is located at the market several blocks west of the Alamo and River Walk. Food, music, and ambiance are all very good. I wouldn't want a steady diet of Tex-Mex food or music, but certainly enjoy it when I get the chance.

On our visits we did not just spend time in San Antonio, but often got up early to make short trips out of town. Day trips were made up into the hill country stopping at a winery, and we just had to see Luckenbach (I didn't see Waylon or Willie). Another was to see a giant sinkhole near Hondo where the Hondo River is diverted to during high flow times to recharge the aquifer that supplies most of San Antonio's water. A couple of visits down to border towns were memorable.

Leaving early, we headed to Eagle Pass and visited Piedras Negras across the Rio Grande. In early September it is still hot in south Texas, so I decided that rather than walk, we could ride the bus across. Even close to the border, almost everybody was of Mexican descent, and on the bus we were the only Anglos. Even better, as we walked the town square we were still the only Anglos out that early.

Diane was hesitant because it seemed everybody she saw spoke a language she couldn't understand. It was her first time in such a situation. She was nervous at the prospect of this trip and about backed out on taking the bus ride to cross the border. It wasn't a big deal to me, as I had lived for almost two years where I couldn't understand much of what was said, plus had spent time working with the migrant farm laborers that came to harvest tobacco at our place.

There were not near the number and diversity of shops that you find in Laredo or other border towns, but Diane did manage to get a deal on a fake Dooney purse that lasted for years, as well as a pair of *gold* loop earrings.

Another visit was to Laredo when my friend Roy Toney and his wife, Essie, went with us for the long weekend to San Antonio. Now Diane is a shopper on occasion, but she can't hold a candle to Roy or Essie. After an hour I had shopped about all I needed to (and bought nothing), so I adjourned to a small outside bar in the square. That afternoon was enjoyable, sucking down Tecata and exchanging lies with an off-duty police sergeant.

DIANE, ROY AND ESSIE TAKE IN THE ALAMO

San Antonio remains a place I like to visit. Like New Orleans the cuisine, sounds, and culture are just enough different to offer a real change of pace from your normal life.

TRAVELING
WITH CHARLIE

It seems like there is a famous book with about the same name. But instead of a dog, this is about our travels with our youngest son, Charles. He has always been really fun to travel with. Even as a young child, he stayed interested in seeing where we were going and noticing almost everything we passed by or visited. His brothers could sleep for miles and miles, but it seemed Charlie was afraid he would miss something.

Before he graduated from high school, he joined the Army Reserve, doing his basic training between his junior and senior year. After graduation he attended language school in Monterey, California, and a communications school near San Angelo, Texas. He took up bicycling and rode miles at both postings.

We still do not know exactly what he did. All he said was he worked with radios and maps. Later he became an instructor at Fort Devin, Massachusetts, during several summers. We did go up for a visit with him and my brother Jim, who lived just a few miles away. On that first visit we came to the post gate and asked where his unit was located. They didn't know of any such unit.

A friend of ours was also an instructor there and also an avid ham operator. There was no missing his truck covered with antennas. When all the check-in procedures were complete we just drove around the post. Finally, in a back, out of the way corner we spotted the truck. It was parked in front of a compound with a twenty-foot fence, topped with concertina wire around a no window, block building. And we still don't know what they did.

SUMMER 1995

Charles worked full time at the University of Kentucky for eight years, first on the farm crew, then as a supply buyer, and finally in their computer hardwire division. All that time he was also a part time student in computer science. He actually finished his degree at a few years younger than I had. He is now a teacher at a technical school.

In that summer of 1995 he had a couple of weeks' vacation, and we asked him to go camping with us in Canada. By June 29 Diane was again wrapping up four weeks of summer school. That morning we got loaded up and took care of unfinished business. Picking up Charlie after lunch, it was north we went.

Hoping to make it well into Canada that night, we stuck to I-75 all the way to the crossing at Windsor. We crossed the border, stopped for currency exchange, made a beer run for real Blue, and got fresh fruit. It was close to seven in the evening when we set up in Wheatley Provincial Park, which is located on Lake Erie about sixty miles into Ontario. We had made good time, gotten through Toledo before rush hour, and had driven in the opposite direction of Detroit rush hour traffic. This year our transportation was a rental van, which we kept for almost three weeks, because we also used it to go to a family reunion in North Carolina. My old pickup was getting too beat up, and Diane's Dakota was too small for more than just the two of us. In three weeks I put over four thousand miles on that van.

That night there were storms and rain; however, we were now pretty experienced at foul weather camping. Plus, I don't think we much more than heard them, because we were worn out from a long day. The morning dawned clear and was beautiful for a ride along Lake Eire on Route 3.

A short stop was made at Del Haven orchard and farm market to visit with Hector DeLange. I had visited with Mr. DeLange on a Cattlemen's tour, and it turns out he had Kentucky ties during his working career, and we knew several people in common. For years he had been a burley tobacco buyer for Canadian tobacco companies while in Kentucky and was also a grower of flue-cured tobacco, along with having a peach orchard.

For those that don't know, Kentucky is the burley tobacco capital of the world. It is the addition of burley to cigarettes that gives them the unique American blend taste that seems to be preferred around the world. Burley can be grown many places around the world; however, we have a unique climate for the air curing and aging process. The warm, dry days and cool, humid nights of early fall have so far not been duplicated. In spite of a decline in tobacco use, it is still an important force in our economy.

Leaving Del Haven, we wandered east with the goal to camp just short of Niagara and visit the falls. It was early afternoon when we stopped at Chippewa Conservation Area just about twenty miles west of the falls. It was here that the true hospitality of the Canadian people, especially in Ontario, showed up. It was the day before Canada Day (their Fourth of July), and the campground was actually full. The manager took pity on us, opened up what is usually a group-only site for us, and even had a table there before we could get set up.

As experienced tent campers, it rarely takes us more than a few minutes to get settled—usually not much more time than checking in to a motel and getting luggage unloaded and into a room. All set, it was off to see the falls. Charles was only three years old when we visited it many years before, and he had no real memory of that visit. Niagara Falls is another of nature's wonders, and even if a very touristy place, is well worth visiting and even revisiting. Lots of people think only in terms it being a final destination, but for me it is a good stop for a while, but not the shops and tourist trappings in the town.

One of the things we did for the first time is to take the tunnel to view the falls from somewhat below. The roar, the mist, the rainbows, and the awesome volume of water is mind-boggling. I have visited both the American and Canadian sides, but I personally prefer the Canadian.

DIANE AND I ENJOY THE SPRAY FROM NIAGARA FALLS

Again, that night there was rain, but not near as much as the previous night. The worst thing about rain camping is making sure that everything is packed and put away so that what is wet doesn't soak everything else. The key is to make sure the tent is the last thing down so everything else stays dry by getting it rolled up and put into storage bags and containers while still dry. In our long-bed truck there is always room to put the tent separate, but in the van it was a little harder with two tents.

Our goal for the day, which happened to be Canada Day, was to get to the Ottawa area and see the celebration, concert, and fireworks that night on Parliament Hill. The plan was to cross in to Quebec and stay at Gatineau Provincial Park, but it proved to be full. For that night we ended up with a suite for a bargain rate at a Ramada Inn close to the Rideau Canal and a not too long of a walk to Parliament Hill. You do get lucky sometimes. Want to have a fun time? Spend it with nearly 200,000 Canadians at a concert and fireworks in Ottawa. Diane's comment in her log was, "Wild!"

Early the next morning, we headed to Byward Market for breakfast and taking in all the fresh market stuff. When we had walked the market and Parliament Hill, and had taken in the changing of the guard, we headed to Quebec.

QUEBEC SUCKS!

While Diane and I had thoroughly enjoyed our visit in Quebec City the year before, it was not to be this time. I had heard about and seen pictures of Mont Tremblant and wanted to visit and camp there. It is as beautiful as advertised.

By mid-afternoon we were in our campsite and settled in. Now I must explain that while checking in the young lady who handled us went to college in Indiana and spoke good English. In filling out the paperwork, I indicated that we had two tents, one for us and a smaller one for my son. All was okay, and she said it was no problem.

Charles and I decided it would be neat to canoe the lake for a couple of hours, and we did while Diane took in the scenery as she looked up from her book. We were having a great time in a beautiful place.

Following supper and showers, we settled in for a cool, good night's sleep, when it happened. We saw rangers ride around several times that evening. About twenty-five minutes before dark, a young man on a bicycle stopped and told me we could not have two tents set up on one site.

Huh? I explained we had checked in, told the ranger our camp setup, and had been told it was okay. He insisted that two setups were not acceptable.

When I pointed to two nearby sites, one with a motor home and tent, and the other with a tent camper and tent, his reply was, "They are families."

My patience was wearing thin at that point. I was tired and about ready for bed. At that point he called for reinforcements. His supervisor showed up with the same contentions. I showed him my son's birth certificate, but he insisted we couldn't be considered a family, as he was over twenty-one. His compromise: we could take down the small tent and Charles could sleep with us, or he could move to another campground a few miles away. Our small tent had barely enough room for us, let alone another big, strapping two hundred-pounder, and I certainly didn't want to drive five miles and set up a tent in the dark. Final answer: either do one of those or leave. Totally pissed off, I told him where he could stick his campground, packed up, and left. Now I am not always a big fool, just sometimes. I had noticed a car waiting about seventy-five yards up the road. Guess what? When I looped back after loading and leaving, that very car was setting up a camp on my now unoccupied one. Enough said. *Quebec sucks!* Or at least members of their officialdom do. Even after a letter to their department of tourism, they offered no explanation or apology. In no place in their printed material or park's website rules could I find a reference to any such rule.

In the small hours of the morning, we checked in to a motel in Hawksberry, Ontario. I have since driven across a corner of Quebec, but do not plan to ever spend more time than necessary there, and definitely not one dime, unless absolutely unavoidable

Leaving Hawksberry the next morning, we dropped down to Cornwall and crossed into New York. Back in to the United States! The route we took was east on US 11 across the upper end of Lake Champlain and through the Green Mountains on route 104, until we picked up US 2 near St. Johnsbury, Vermont. From there it was just a short hop to Moose Brook State Park, New Hampshire, where we had stayed several times before. The beautiful, relaxing drive had served to take the edge off the experience the night before, but I still think Quebec sucks.

It was the Fourth of July celebration time in Gorham, New Hampshire. We again spent the evening in the small New England town, complete with a fair, concert, and fireworks—a thoroughly enjoyable experience. And we have been back a couple more times.

We had originally planned to head across to visit the Bay of Fundy, but the boondoggle in Quebec had thrown us off our route and timing. We ended up crossing Maine on side roads to end up at Camden Hill State Park where we had stayed before. This time we decided to stay a couple of nights.

Having arrived before lunch, it was seafood time. After a great clam roll lunch sitting by the bay, it was off on another adventure. After lunch we did a touristy thing. Boarding the schooner Appledore, it was off for a couple of hours cruise out into the Penobscot Bay. While this may not be an adventure for coastal dwellers, it was for this landlubber from Kentucky. We did learn that even if the day was warm close on shore, a light jacket felt good out on the forty-five degree water.

On the way back to the campground, a stop at a local seafood outlet yielded three mid-sized lobsters for supper. There's nothing like a lobster feast at your campsite. It was a beautiful end to a great day. I don't know if the smell of lobster did it or if it was pure luck, but that night we had a visitor.

Shortly after we went to bed, Diane woke me up and said, "Something is out there."

Now, when she says that it means, *get up and go take a look*. At home, if the dogs bark and she says, "I wonder what they are barking at?" and it means the same thing. *Go look!*

Peering out of the tent, I spied a raccoon and sleepily said, "It's just a coon," but she had to look more.

We do a good job of putting things up out of the way of invading critters, but this one just kept poking around. Now awake and armed with a bright light, I took a closer look, not just a glance through sleep-hazed eyes. What I saw looked almost like a small bear disguised as a raccoon. With its big silver back, it could have been the granddaddy of all raccoons. Thankfully, though big, he wasn't the troublemaker that the high IQ coon was in Florida. With a little noise and light shining, he wandered off, but to this day that is the biggest damn coon I have ever seen.

The next day we rediscovered the very inexpensive but enjoyable past time of riding out to coastal islands on the Maine ferry system. This time we rode the

Rockland-Vinalhaven ferry. Going just as a passenger, the cost is almost negligible, and the scenery is great. Arriving at Vinalhaven, we proceeded to take a walking tour, do some window-shopping, and just enjoy the R&R. Sea air and walking is great for the appetite. A lunch of seafood chowder and crab rolls hit the spot. Riding the ferry back, it was all I could do to keep my eyes open. Unless I am driving, all I have to do is get a full belly and relax to head off to dreamland, no matter where I happen to be.

That evening we went up on top of Mount Battle, which is part of the park. With an exceptionally clear evening, we could see to the horizon both ways, probably twenty-five miles or more. It was beautiful with the harbor at our feet and blue ocean everywhere, with scattered islands in the distance. The two days at Camden remain a cherished memory for us and for Charles.

However, all good trips have an end point. With an early start, we ended up at Rome, New York, in a motel and managed to drop a few dollars at the Turning Stone Casino. Then we had a great drive across the state through wine, orchard, and dairy country, finally ending up camping one more night at Geneva State Park on Lake Eire. That left a fairly easy drive home the next day.

To me, being able to travel and camp with my youngest son, Charles, as a young adult is something I will cherish all of my life. He is a joy to travel with and super to camp with, and is always interested in seeing new things and having new experiences. At this point he has two young children and stays tied up at home, but maybe sometime again we can make another journey, but with some added passengers.

It ended up that we had one more journey to make with Charles. During the next year's spring break, he joined us on our trek to camp at St. Joseph State Park on Cape San Blas in the panhandle of Florida. At least this year the high IQ coon didn't harass us.

I did one more travel thing for Charlie. Like my father sent his mother and I on a great trip for a honeymoon, I did the same for him. After his time in Monterey, California, at the Defense Language School he had often mentioned wanting to revisit there. For a wedding present, I arranged for a flight and rooms in the San Francisco area. It was in doing this that I first got hooked up with using Jack London Inn in Oakland as a base of operation in that area. I found it while trying to keep cost down and still be in a fairly decent place. My friend Roy had two sisters who teach there, so he had them check it out before I booked it. I will tell more about this place in a later side-trip story.

THE TOUR GUIDE

This seems like a good time to take a break from what have been basically personal or family travels. For twenty-five years I have organized tours for our local Cattle Association and helped plan training tours for my regional coworkers. During that time, we visited forty-five US states, four Canadian Provinces, and Mexico.

I had a cohort in planning the trips and lining up the visits we made. Roy Toney served as the local district conservationist for NRCS. Between my contacts in the cattle business and his from serving on a national program review committee all over the United States, there are few places that at least one of us don't have personal contacts to assist in arranging farm visits.

The program was actually started with a two-fold purpose. One goal was to broaden the knowledge and vision of our local farm leaders. The other was to build a higher level of rapport between the local leadership and us.

I could list several ideas and mindset changes that occurred as a result, but will offer only one example. In the early years we still had several dairies, and a significant income was derived from the calves raised to be sold either as feeder calves or replacement cows. Many of them had health issues, raising baby calves with lots of respiratory diseases. One dairy in particular was losing almost 20 percent of its calves. While on a tour, this producer saw baby calves being raised in outside hutches, with the hutches set on a bed of a large rock for drainage. Bringing this idea home, his death loss dropped to less than 3 percent, which for him translated in to almost ten thousand dollars a year in additional income. And this doesn't even factor in the awful feeling that all of us have when we lose what are almost family members.

As far as bringing our leadership together, the tours have exceeded our hopes. There's nothing like listening as conversations flow freely riding along in a van. The farmers themselves renewed and built new ties and friendships along the way. As with many people in today's world, we are all always too busy to do much more than sit in on a two-hour meeting. Farmers are always reluctant to escape even for a few days, but would justify going on an educational tour.

Make no mistake, these were not vacations but true learning experiences beyond a normal trip. It used to really bother me when somebody that had never been on one of Roy and my tours would ask, "Where are you taking them on vacation this year?"

A typical day started at six in the morning and sometimes didn't end until almost dark or after. During that day, two to four hours were on the roads with the rest occupied with visits to farm operations, research farms, processing plants, and even in a classroom. It was fun, but also really educational and often tiring.

I mentioned how many states we visited on our cattlemen trips. Recently, before we got too senile, Roy and I sat down with a large map and put markers where we could remember stops or visits we made over the years. While we are still adding markers, the count has reached over 120 in forty-three states, four Canadian provinces, and two Mexican states. And often there are multiple tour stops in one marker area. We have visited over four hundred farms/ranches, processing plants, and research stations. The next step is to mark our routes on a roadmap. We hit a lot of gray roads and several not-even-on-a-map roads.

Probably the most outstanding feature of doing a trip like we do is the local contacts with people we made and the insight we get in to the local agriculture, landscapes, and culture.

As one of the participants said to me, "I have done a lot of traveling, even visiting some of the areas we have, but never really got to know what I was visiting."

By the way, over the years a few people have made most of the trips, but at last count about two hundred different people have made a farm tour with me.

THE FIRST TRIP

Roy and I did not plan an ambitious tour for our first effort. It was a simple swing up in to Ohio to see some new grass varieties, grazing, and a cattle water system, plus a stop in Indiana to visit the Eli Lilly animal research facility east of Indianapolis. We could only convince three to go with us, but it was a success, and by the next year we had a fifteen-passenger vanload. As the years passed our numbers increased and we took two, then three or more vans on our tours. The largest number we ever took was fifty-seven people, but we averaged around thirty.

You noticed I mentioned using vans rather than a bus, even as our groups grew larger. There were reasons. We did not want to lose the intimacy of the van. Often we would travel longer or on roads where a bus couldn't practically go. A big reason was for the farmers we visited; we did not want our host to provide transportation around the ranch or farm, and we got to see a lot more because we were able to go off-road. I have often wondered that if the rental companies really knew where we took their vans, if they would ever rent to us again. More than once we had to get out and push.

LONGEST TOUR

For the ninth tour we got really ambitious. Roy and I planned a twelve-day trip out to Montana with lots of stops along the way. We really thought that the group would be such a short number that we would have to cancel. But it turned out that twenty-two wanted to make the grand tour.

Some four thousand plus miles later, having passed through twelve states with stops in all but those adjoining Kentucky, we did it. Surprisingly, only the first and last days were actually all-day drives. At least every day a stop was made in the morning and another in the afternoon, and on some days stops took up most of the day. There were several highlights on this tour.

Our route took us through Indiana, Illinois, Wisconsin, Minnesota, South Dakota, Wyoming, Montana, Idaho, Utah, Colorado, Kansas, and Missouri. Along the route we were introduced to the tall grass prairie, sugar beets, potatoes, mint, lots of cows, and much more.

One of the highlights for me was a visit to Jorgenson Ranch in central South Dakota, which is a diversified family operation spanning four generations. The senior member, Martin Jorgenson, was a leader in beef cattle improvement in both genetics and financial management. Much of today's Angus genetics trace to an origin in that herd. Their operation is well diversified, with not just cattle, but also hogs and a hunting enterprise.

Another of the best memories is our trek across the Big Horn Mountains with their huge expanse of open range mountain pastures with large herds grazing along the roadside, and we saw a seventy-year-old wrestle in the snow with a forty-year-old. We dropped down from the mountains to visit a combined cattle ranch and sugar beet operation. Not only are beets still a big source of sugar, but the tops are also great feed for the cowherd.

After the visit east of Powell, Wyoming, we headed to stay the night at the Buffalo Bill Cabins in Cody. I noted earlier in this story that in recent years they have been upgraded and modernized, but at that time they were really basic. Our philosophy over the years was to go as inexpensively as possible. As long as the room was clean and the beds were not too bad, that was okay. After all, we were just going to spend a few hours, take a shower, and move on. A great source to find good, inexpensive lodging has been the people we are going to visit and our local contacts. Often they know of a good, locally owned place that I can't find on the Internet or in travel guides.

Even though it was the middle of July and we had been enjoying the mid-80s and low humidity, we were not prepared for Saturday night at the rodeo in Cody. As we left Powell, we hit a rain shower that evidently was the edge of a summer cold front. By the time we had supper, a light jacket felt good.

It was Saturday night, and since I was the only one of the group to have taken in a western rodeo, I had gotten tickets for the group. When we left the cabins, the wind was blowing and temperatures were in the upper 40s— almost too much even for a light jacket. Never fear, we were innovative. A quick stop back in the room and the beds were stripped of their wool blankets, and away we went. I don't know what they thought at the rodeo gate, and we really didn't care that we were the only ones entering the rodeo like we would a November football game back home. Even with the blankets, it felt like frostbite was setting in by the bull riding, and the wind had reached above 25 mph with the temperatures in the upper 30s. That proved to be a togetherness evening, but we stuck it out to the end. It was definitely the coldest time we ever had, even though we have toured well up in to November at other times.

Leaving Cody on Sunday morning, it was a day of doing the tourist thing with a drive-through of

Yellowstone National Park. Like many of the places we visited, Roy and I were the only ones that had been there before. This time our route took us northwest up Route 296 joining US 212 near Cooke City, Montana, and in through the Silver Gate. This route took us through Dead Indian Pass, rather than up the longer route to Red Lodge, then down through Beartooth Pass, which, I think, is the more awesome way to the Silver Gate. At that time, the road through Dead Indian Pass had not been improved, but was full of steep switchbacks and was slow going. Part of it was even still gravel, whereas today it is an improved blacktop road.

Shortly after winding down out of the forested hills and along the river, we spied the first buffalo in the distance. In spite of Roy and my insistence that there would be all kinds of opportunities to see lots more buffalo all day, nothing would stop the group from hiking almost a mile to get a closer look. Reflecting back, I guess I had forgotten the youthful exuberance you feel when experiencing something for the first time. Easily the most excited was the seventy-year-old who was seeing buffalo in the wild for the first time.

For the rest of the day we did what would best be described as the highlights-only tour of Yellowstone. They just got a sampler taste. On a later tour, we did schedule an entire weekend in Yellowstone. Most of our sightseeing visits have always been scheduled on the weekends. We preferred not to impose on our hosts on a weekend.

Leaving Yellowstone through the north gate at nearly dark, we spent the night in Livingston and saddled up early the next morning for another visit I had been looking forward to for a while. Leachman Angus, operated by Les Leachman and his son Jay, was another of the top genetic sources in the world for Angus cattle.

Les is a legend in cattle-breeding circles. His story begins at Ohio State University at the end of World War II, where he and his brother Lee, along with several others, destined to determine the course of the cattle industry for over half of a century, went to school. In the period of about four years, there were future department chairs, deans, sales managers, and numerous ranch mangers all in school together. Les was as highly respected for his knowledge and management as anyone in the cattle industry. I was fortunate enough to cross paths with Les, and even co-owned a National Western Champion bull from his outfit years before. So nothing would do, while in the neighborhood, but to spend a morning looking at great Angus cattle and swapping stories. And I had enough sense to listen most of the time.

Visiting this ranch was where the absolute importance of water all across the west first hit home. On many subsequent visits west, water rights, limits, controls, and regulations has been a reoccurring theme on most visits. Water is a very serious consideration and expense, basically unknown here in the east.

That afternoon we got to see our first goldmine; the Sunlight Mine near Whitehall is a really interesting operation. At first approach, it looks just like a pretty big hole in the side of a mountain. Then at our first overlook, we noticed that the large ore trucks with tires twice the height of a tall man looked like a kid's small toy on the mine floor, and our perceptions changed. Returning there a couple of years ago, Diane and I had the good fortune to spend some time with their geologist, which for science-type people was more than just interesting.

DIANE IN THE SHOVEL AT GOLD MINE

After a couple of other local ranch visits, we pulled in to Dillon, Montana, for the night. During that long daylight time of year in the north, it can make for a long, tiring day if you start shortly after dawn and end shortly before dark.

Up and out early the next morning, we stopped at the US National Sheep Research Station near Dubois, Idaho, and then went on down to Rexburg, Idaho. Our contact at Rexburg was the county agent for Madison County Gale

Harding. Gale has spent most of his career as the extension agent there and really knows the land and the people. I had been to Rexburg a few times before, but until we spent late morning and the afternoon with him I really didn't know much about the place, except it was a pretty neat town surrounded by lots of farming.

Gale first took us up to the foothill bench east of the town that was covered with those famous Idaho spuds. Potato farming, as we learned, is an extremely high investment crop with great rewards sometimes and great risk of loss at others. Many of the farmers have several $100,000 harvesters, trucks, and large cool storage barns. That year the farm we visited was looking at a net of over $300,000 for his crop. Sounds great, doesn't it? However, we visited again twelve years later and that same farmer was looking at a loss of over $300,000. A few pennies price drop, an early frost that destroys quality and makes the potato unfit for use, and numerous other factors can wipe out two years profit in a few days.

I have stayed in loose contact with Gale over the years, and he is still the knowledgeable, entertaining host as always. The only real crisis ever within our group occurred during our first visit with Gale; therefore, he has never forgotten us. One of the younger participants either had taken the wrong dose or forgotten his blood pressure medicine. The combination of high altitude, long days, and rich food finally got to him. He actually was showing some signs of a potential heart attack or stroke problems. It proved that his blood pressure was dangerously high.

Thankfully, Gale knew his way around and was able to get him in to see the right specialist. After some high-powered drugs and resting while we toured, everything was pretty much under control, and he didn't have to be hospitalized. We have been fortunate over the years that this was the only serious incident to ever occur while on a tour.

The next day we were off to Utah. We had no idea that just north of Salt Lake City there was a thriving horticulture industry. That day we visited a greenhouse with acres under glass for rose production, vegetable fields, and bedding plant growers, plus a visit to the Great Salt Lake. I can honestly say that in spite of the lake, the beautiful capital, and church, Salt Lake City is someplace I really don't want to visit and spend time in. After seeing parks and streets occupied by homeless people and police pulling a body out of the dumpster beside our hotel the next morning, it just didn't appear my kind of a place. It kind of reminded me of the impressions I have of Dallas, Houston, New York, or Boston. There was some neat stuff there, but the downside outweighs the upside for me.

Heading east the next day after a short stop at Dinosaur National Monument, we had a great stop in Moffat County, Colorado. The 50,000-acre ranch, located near the small crossroads town of Maybell, turned out to be a great host. Driving back five miles on dirt tracks, we saw antelope, deer, and lots of other wildlife before finally finding his cows. The whole ranch in that arid, great basin, high plain could carry only about five hundred mother cows and their calves. It requires about one hundred acres per cow and the cows regularly rotate themselves around the large ranch to fresh grass. Our group, like me many years before, was almost dumfounded how cows could stay so fat and slick with so little apparent feedstuff, but they did.

The outback visit was just a little of what made this a great stop. Returning to the ranch headquarters, there was an early supper on the grill waiting for us. In addition, neighboring ranchers, some from fifty plus miles away, had come to join us for fellowship. Those situations are a lot of what makes this type of tour so good.

We stayed too long, but hated to leave good company and ended up getting to our motel in Steamboat Springs at almost eleven at night. Early the next morning, I introduced the group to the Lone Moose Café in Kremling, and everybody agreed that that may have had bigger pancakes or better sweet rolls, but couldn't remember where or when.

Wrapping up this tour was pretty much of a drive home with a couple of Kansas stops to see sunflowers and oil seed processing. Mostly, we just wanted to get home by that point. After two decades this tour is still considered one of the top three we have taken.

THE BEST TOUR

Our tours are kind of like sex: all good, but some better than others. When we were on the long trip, one of the men made the comment that when we were so far west, why didn't we just go on to California? Four years later we did plan a tour that took in California. And after it was complete, maybe I should have stopped then while I was at the top of my game.

As we go through this tour, keep in mind that the total cost per person was $450, which included airfare, van cost, and rooms. In addition, the cattlemen we visited fed us several times, and all but one motel had a free breakfast. One of the participants later told me that both he and his wife combined had spent less than $1,100 for the nine-day tour. A friend of mine has a travel agency, and he priced a similar tour at almost $1500 per person.

Flying out of Louisville early in the morning, we arrived in Salt Lake City at eleven o'clock Mountain Daylight Time, picked up our vans, and headed toward Twin Falls, Idaho. There was a visit set up for supper and a twilight visit to Mon Reposa Ranch near there. Mon Reposa Ranch was located just a few miles west of Twin Falls at Filier.

Years before, I had learned a lesson about taking a group west. That time, while planning to leave shortly after six in the morning, a knock came on the door at three-thirty. One of our travelers had both his watch and biological clock still set on Eastern Standard Time. So it was, that this time we made an evening ranch visit that ended around eleven at night EDT. Nobody knocked on the door at three-thirty the next morning.

Mon Reposa had at one time been a major player in Angus genetics and still had many good cattle. Dr Jim Miller, an engineering professor at the University of Michigan, now owned it. One of the unique things he did was to control the ranch's irrigation systems from his computer in Ann Arbor. At that time, they had the longest circular pivot irrigation system in Idaho. Cattle were being grazed on land too rough or steep for crop farming.

The ranch was located along the canyon of the Snake River. It was here that we got to see the numerous springs flowing out of the northern sidewalls developing into waterfalls down into the river. The water for these springs evidently originates near the Yellowstone Park area and flows underground to emerge at the Snake River Canyon. The water flows underground through porous volcanic rock and tunnels. It seems that the *hot spot* underlying Yellowstone has stayed fairly stationary, while the North American continent has drifted over it. The volcanic area appears to be moving east, but in reality it is the continent moving west.

Following the side roads west on the south side of the Snake River, we rejoined I-84 near Fruitland. It was a really interesting, early morning drive taking in land much different than we were used to around home. Our goal was to reach Thomas Angus Ranch near Baker City, Oregon, shortly before noon. We arrived at 11:45 a.m. and found that a great meal awaited us, prepared by the local cattle association. Over the years, we have prided ourselves that when there is a time to be some place, we are there usually just a few minutes early. In all the tours I can remember, we missed only twice by more than ten minutes. Thomas Angus is another very famous Angus ranch. Bob Thomas had some ties to Kentucky, in that he had worked with the CV Whitney herd that was located just north of Lexington. Even though he primarily worked with the New York unit, he had spent quite a bit of time here in Kentucky. The Thomas Ranch is a large ranch by our standards that is operated with his family, particularly his son Rob. They are a little unusual, in that 100 percent of all their income is derived from cattle sales. Most places are more diversified or have off-farm income. Thomas Ranch sinks or swims by how well their cattle sell. After lunch and fellowship with local cattle ranchers, we visited cows, pastures, and hay that make up their operation.

The following day was a Sunday, and we have never made a Sunday farm visit, so it was a driving tour that day. After the night at Pendleton, Oregon, we crossed the Columbia River to drive Washington Route 14 along the north side of the Columbia Gorge. One of the advantages of traveling by vans is the independence of movement by each one. On a day like this, every van went a little different route, crisscrossing the river and stopping when the mood hit. Each van had a navigator that knew where we were supposed to be and when. Very few screw-ups have ever occurred.

A great example of this happened a couple of years ago in California. Our last stop of the day was in the Cholame Hills on a ranch and our room reservations were in Monterey. We actually departed as much as twenty minutes apart, and at least three vans took slightly different routes and had a little over two-hours drive to reach the motel. As we pulled off the freeway in toward the motel, we met one from the south, one from the east, and the last followed me in from the north. This scenario has happened quite often, even if we didn't see each other for most of a day.

I would rate the drive down the Columbia River gorge as one of the top ten I have ever made. This temperate rain forest is simply beautiful with lots to stop and see. It was just too bad that we could not spend more time exploring.

VISITING THE YAKIMAS

Roy Toney, my fellow tour planner in his travels as part of the national NRCS review committee, has met with agriculture professionals across the nation. One of the contacts he had was with the extension people from the Yakima Nation in Washington State. In 1998 we planned a tour where we would fly in to Seattle, then make a loop up in to British Columbia, Alberta, back in to western Montana/northern Idaho, and make a final stop with the Yakima Nation in Washington.

Most of us had never had a real sit down, person-to-person visit with Native Americans. The Yakima are a very pro-active tribe and are very plainspoken about the rotten deal they have suffered. The Yakima Nation never fought against the United States and has a treaty with the US that predates the state of Washington. It specifies what land belongs to them. This appeared to be a pretty good argument to restore land to the tribe. It won't happen, but they are trying to regain at least some. I doubt that the city of Seattle will be deeded back to them.

Just the interpersonal exchange was well worth the stop, but on this visit was a very unusual visit with a farmer. The tribe had the idea to grow tobacco and develop their own brand of organic Native American cigarettes to sell in the lucrative West coast, yuppie market.

As we walked around the barn to view his tobacco patch, our group's mouths about dropped open. All our farmers either had been or were active tobacco growers. What they saw were tobacco plants just getting started in mid-July and planted in rows eight feet wide. Our tobacco is put in the field right after the frost danger has passed and it is spaced about eighteen inches apart in rows that are about three and a half feet wide. In addition, there were at least four types of tobacco planted in the field. Most people don't realize that there are many different types of tobacco, each with a different purpose for use in a cigarette, cigar, pipe, snuff, or chewing tobacco, and even some are grown for a very pure protein extract.

We immediately had thirty tobacco experts for the farmer to visit with. He had used only very old USDA publications for information. I followed up with their extension people over the next couple of years, and they improved their production techniques. I really don't know how well the marketing went, but I suspect that, as with many new agriculture ventures, success depends on the marketing phase.

For lunch that day they fed us fresh caught salmon prepared to perfection, and we had one of their almost Shaman-like legends visit with us as well. Great day!

By mid-afternoon we arrived at Seaside, Oregon, on the coast. Three of our younger travelers thought it would be great to take a swim in the Pacific. Being brave, they ran to jump in just as they might have in Florida or Myrtle Beach. Luckily, none of them passed out or had a heart attack. Forty-degree water can be shocking to the system. I actually thought they jumped back out much quicker than they went in—they kind of looked like a cartoon.

Monday morning, with an early start, we had breakfast with a group of farmers in the Willamette Valley at Forest Grove, Oregon, before visiting grass seed production, dairies, and more. After these interesting visits, we drove down I-5 to spend the night at Grants Pass, Oregon.

Again, we had an early start south the next day. That ride on a clear day with the snow-capped, dormant volcano peaks is beautiful.

STOPPED FOR SPEEDING

Four vans were rolling south on I-5 with mine in the lead. We usually move on at or slightly above the legal limit. Somehow we missed the entering of a construction zone sign and we weren't passing anybody. In the rearview mirror a flashing blue light appeared in pursuit. California's finest rolled right past the last van and pulled behind our third van with his siren wailing.

Quickly, I told my driver, "Do *not* stop unless he actually waves us over!"

So we roll on.

Later the story came out. An airplane clocked us. California's finest completed the ticketing routine, and the driver of the stopped van could just see the new points on his license with insurance rates going up. Luckily, the trooper took pity on the farm boys, marking them as 5 mph over, not the ten that was the real amount. Results were a mail-in fifty-five dollar fine with no points.

But that wasn't the funny part. The officer asked them if all the vans were traveling together.

"Yes."

The officer's next comment was, "Well, will they wait for you?"

The van driver replied, "You don't know them; they never wait for anybody," and he was right.

California's finest just about lost it laughing. It cost us $1.50 each to pay the fine, and we had lots of dollars' worth of fun harassing the driver.

■

Shortly before noon, we arrived at Tehama Angus Ranch just south of Red Bluff, California. Again, their local cattlemen were waiting for us with grilled tri tip this time.

If you have never had tri tip, you need to. It is generally not available here in the east, but is a preferred grilling cut in California.

That afternoon we visited with the Borror family of Tehama Angus. They are a diversified operation with almonds and olives, in addition to a great herd of cattle. Like several ranches I have visited over the years, they had originally come to California as dairy farmers but had transitioned over to beef cattle. They are now into their fourth generation of operation.

The stops in the Sacramento Valley had been set up by their local livestock specialist for us and included another big feed and fellowship with producers that evening. We finally made it to our motel in Williams at about eleven o'clock at night.

The next day it was off to see the Golden Gate and make an evening visit just north of Santa Rosa. Roy and I were about the only ones in our group that had ever been to San Francisco, so it was an eye-opener for most of them. The people in all four vans ended up seeing and doing something slightly different. This was Diane's first visit to San Francisco; she made me promise to bring her back soon for a longer visit, and we have.

My van hit some of the high spots in the city, but I wanted us to visit Muir Woods National Monument as I had never been there. Muir Woods is another of nature's wonders. Walking through them is as impressive as any great cathedral in the world. Not only did I have that look of wonder on my face, but each of us did that day.

CALIFORNIA SIDE TRIPS

A couple years after the cattlemen's trip to California, Diane's school started to have a fall break in addition to a spring break. Earlier in the year, we had planned a long holiday weekend trip out to Nebraska for a visit with our son and grandson. Sometimes when you book a Friday afternoon flight well before a holiday weekend or school break, it can often result in an overbooked flight that offers a future flight voucher for taking a bump. This time it worked. For taking the bump, we received a flight voucher, a room for the night, and a fifty-dollar food coupon, plus first class seats the next morning. We ended up getting to our son's home the next day only a couple of hours later than our original plan. What is given for taking a bump now is not as lucrative as it was several years ago, but if I don't have a critical schedule I still try.

My friend Roy Toney was almost a champion at getting free trips for taking bumps. Each time, while he was traveling around the United States for his national committee assignment, he would book flights at times that he knew had a high likelihood of being overbooked. At one time, he must have had at least five free r round trip vouchers.

So with a free round trip voucher in hand, Diane and I decided to use it for a trip back to San Francisco. It was earlier in that year we had sent Charles there for his honeymoon trip and decided to again use the Jack London Inn in Oakland for our stay.

We left after school on Thursday afternoon, landing in San Francisco at nine o'clock in the evening Pacific Time. Since then, whenever fares are equal I fly in to Oakland, as it is a lot easier to get around than San Francisco's airport. The Jack London Inn in Oakland is certainly not a four-star facility, but I have found the rooms clean, the staff helpful, and the location wonderful. I really like visiting San Francisco, but each time I find it really pleasant to get back to the laidback atmosphere around Jack London Square.

It is also very easy to get around the entire bay from the square in Oakland. The ferry is a block away, the bay area rapid transit is a few blocks away, and the freeway is just a couple of blocks. The city of Oakland is doing a great job of revitalizing the downtown area. Should you want to head east, it's possible to be out to the valleys in less than an hour, and it's even easy to swing north to Napa and avoid much of the San Francisco traffic—even getting over to the coast at Half Moon Bay is not too bad.

Three things that I really consider neat and unusual about staying at the Jack London Inn are: the Amtrak, the produce terminal, and the farmers market. A main rail line runs right down the center of the main street in front of the hotel and includes the coastal Amtrak line. It does have some noise associated with it, but after all, it's in the middle of a major port city, and it adds to the flavor.

The produce terminal is something else. About three in the morning I faintly hear what sounds like construction or trash trucks dumping dumpsters. *What is that noise?* Later that day, I walked up to the corner of the street where the noise seemed to be originating, and there was nothing, just what looked like closed up old buildings. Well, the next night I hear it again. Not to be denied this time, I get dressed and go look. What was abandoned late the previous morning was now a bustling produce terminal with fork lifts, refrigerated trucks, and people everywhere. In those buildings was produce from all over California and the Pacific Basin. I thoroughly enjoyed having coffee and conversation with the vendors. Also, I have come to the conclusion that folks in California keep the best produce for themselves and ship the seconds to us.

Jack London Square has a three-block-long Sunday farmers market. Its growers sell every type of fruit, vegetable, and flower grown in the area. I also have been a grower for a farmer's market and have helped establish a couple, so I have an appreciation for a really good market. I had a great time visiting with the farmers and market manager. It was sort of a busman's holiday.

That first trip we ended up using public transportation whenever we went over to San Francisco, except for a visit to Golden Gate Bridge on our way to Muir Woods. The first two full days after taking the early ferry, we proceeded to explore the city on trolleys, cable cars, and buses. It is relatively inexpensive with transfers, and the local people were always helpful with directions, and they often added stories and details about their city. Maybe we were just lucky, but the locals seemed friendlier than in most big cities we have visited.

We especially enjoyed walking Golden Gate Park, seeing a few old hippies hanging on in Haight Asbury, and taking in the sights and sounds of the tourist traps at Fisherman's Wharf (a little of that goes a long way with me). Other days we drove down to Monterey and into Napa Valley.

We really enjoyed Monterey, even if it is a little touristy. The food is good, the aquarium fabulous, and the coastline spectacular. Plus, it is good to drool over the little houses along the Seventeen Mile Drive. If you are ever in Monterey, try Tarpy's Roadhouse for a meal. It is off the beaten tourist path, but is a local favorite that a motel manager recommended to me.

We have returned a few times to that area when we find exceptional airfares; however, just a couple of years ago we discovered another place that really suits our preferences more.

Airfares were much cheaper flying in to the Ontario airport just east of Los Angeles, and we had a free one-way to use flying back from the San Francisco area. In looking for a place to stay along the coast heading north, I ran across Morro Bay, and it sounded great. It seemed to have a lot of what we were looking for, ocean, good seafood, and not too crowded. I booked us for a couple of nights at the Back Bay Inn in the adjoining town of Baywood Park, and it turned out to be a real find right on the water. It had a great breakfast and a wine/cheese tasting each evening. There was a trail along the bay for great bird watching, as well as eucalyptus groves with thousands of over-wintering Monarch butterflies, and Montana de Oro State Park was just a few minutes' drive. It was just a laidback place to chill for a couple of days of R&R and wasn't too over priced.

The town of Morro Bay may be crowded in the major tourist summer time, but it was not during our trip in mid-February. The weather was wonderful with clear, warm days and cool nights. The marina area had several good seafood restaurants, not fancy and not expensive.

Just eleven miles away is San Luis Obispo where California Polytechnic University is located. Reading about what goes on; it is like many college towns with concerts, plays, and lots of stuff to do. We have now thought that this area may compete with Apalachicola, Florida, for a place to spend a few winter weeks when we decide to finally slow down some. It may sound a long way, but with flying time and using Amtrak or driving it is almost as quick to get there as to the Florida Panhandle and costs are basically equivalent.

■

After leaving Muir Woods, my van drove up Route 1 to Bodega Bay and back across to Santa Rosa to check in to our motel. All four van-groups saw different things, and we swapped stories. All the vans arrived within twenty minutes of each other again.

We had an invitation to a cookout and visit at Oak Ridge Ranch near Callistoga for that evening. The LaFranchi family operates the ranch with Cheryl, a daughter, as the manager. Her family, like the Borrors at Tehama, had moved to California as dairy farmers with an outstanding registered Ayrshire herd.

It was one of the best visits our group had made, and certainly the hospitality was great. The growing wine industry had leased quite a lot of their best cropland for grape production, and their Angus cowherd ran in the hill country around the valley.

Their tenant, Beringer's Winery, had donated some of their best wine, and we had excellent tri tips again. Good fellowship, good people, good food, good wine, and good cattle made for a memorable visit. Returning to our motel late, we were awakened in the middle of the night by a medium-sized earthquake. We have a few small ones around home, but for most, that was their first really noticeable quake. While actually a minor quake for that area, Diane slept in her clothes, plus woke up to check the news several times.

It was time to start back east, but the highlights weren't finished yet. After a drive along Route 12 through wine country, we hooked up with Ken Churches, the county agent in Calaveras County. Yep, the same county as the Great Jumping Frog contest written about by Mark Twain. Ken is a longtime extension agent in that county, and he set up a visit with one of the original California settler's descendants. We joined them at their summer grazing, which is irrigated pasture on the east side of the San Joaquin Valley. As we discovered, they had about the oldest water rights in the valley. As a result, they were able to access irrigation water, even when others are cut off due to shortage, which can be a ranch-saving factor.

Visiting their home in the Sierra foothills near Mountain Ranch, California, we discovered that they had another project. When the first settlers reached California it was almost exclusively made up of land covered with scattered oaks and native species of tall grasses. Over the years, introduced grasses have mostly replaced many of the native species. This family had been able to find some survivors of the native species and was repopulating their winter grazing pastures in the hills with them. This area of California is different, in that its grazing is the opposite of much of the west. Where most western ranchers take cattle to mountain grazing for the summer and valleys for the winter, the ranchers of this part of California move to the valleys for summer and hills for winter. Following a good lesson on the history of grazing in the state, we had another great cookout put on by the local ranchers.

That afternoon it was up and over the Sierras following Route 88 to join US 395 in Nevada. It was a beautiful trip through the hills and forest on what is not a highly traveled road. Our destination was to stay the night in Reno. Personally, I like Reno more than most casino towns. As always, a laidback atmosphere ends up being my favorite.

That evening I thought that maybe my trip planning wasn't too good. In making the reservations I thought that I was talking to the group representative for the Hampton Inn, which is actually a part of the Harrah's complex. It turns out I wasn't. Driving up, we see the Hampton but couldn't find any place to stop, park, and go check in. Up the block there was the Harrah's entrance with an unloading zone. We unloaded and proceeded to drag luggage right through the casino, with strange looks by the patrons as we passed through. Arriving at the Hampton desk, I found no reservations in our group or my name. I almost panicked. What do you do when you need twenty-two rooms at the last minute? Luck was on our side. As I was feeling my blood pressure rise and despair starting to increase, the group representative for Harrah's walks by on her way out the door to go home. Our desk clerk, who was also a friend of the rep, asked her if maybe Harrah's had some rooms, as they were almost sold out at the Hampton. Hearing both my name and our group, she laughed and said she was the one who had my reservations. All was well in the world at this point. Except, right back through the casino all forty-two of us paraded again, dragging the luggage to the increasingly puzzled stares of the same people usually engrossed in their slots and blackjack. Hey, it worked out, and I got a suite as group leader.

The next day proved to be another highlight. Often I get accused of sometimes setting up a fill-in stop just to break up the day, and occasionally they are right, but not this day. Roy had a stop along the Humboldt River where they were working with salt tolerant varieties of Alfalfa. Often the irrigation water on the lower end of a valley system can have a salt buildup as it passes through fields and back in to the system. Plus, the water there naturally has a higher salt content than we experience in the east, and it becomes more concentrated the farther down the stream it travels. An interesting sidelight is that since that time some of these varieties are seeing use to remove and recycle excess nutrients generated by municipal sewage discharge, rather than let it move in to the drainage water.

Following this early morning visit, I had a surprise for the group. What they thought to be just another stop turned in to a very memorable one. TS Ranch near Battle Mountain, Nevada is over two-thirds the size of the state of Rhode Island. The front of the ranch runs over forty miles along I-80. As you drive up to the ranch headquarters, you see 90,000 acres of irrigated alfalfa spreading out behind to mountains in the background. Later we found out that they have another 350,000 acres of dry grazing in the hills.

The TS ranch exists, as it is, for one reason—gold. In the hills there is a gold mine with a major excess water problem. Running down the mountain is a six-foot diameter drainage pipe used to feed the irrigation pivots. The water is actually very pure and is lower in salts than most water in the region. Why not just let it flow in to the Humbolt River to feed ranches and towns downstream who badly need it? Water laws in existence for decades do not allow any water to be moved from its historic accumulation region. So the gold mine has a ranch using irrigation to return the water to its natural accumulation area.

In spite of being owned by a successful gold mine, the ranch still was expected to pull its own weight financially. Their biggest profit center was the sale of alfalfa hay to dairies and horse farms in California.

They could have probably made a larger profit by running fewer cattle, but as the ranch manager said, "We sell hay to make money, but we run cows because at heart we are cowboys."

And cowboys they were in the old sense.

All their handling of the cattle is done as it had been one hundred years before from horseback. They could have done differently with the young cattle running on the irrigated pasture, but the hill land was just too rough for anything but a horse. A ten-year-old cowboy put on a demonstration of working and treating an injured calf the way they do on the range. This calf had become too curious about a porcupine and had a nose full of quills.

After a cookout lunch, we were able to drive back in to the foothills to see some of the mama cows. Once their cows have weaned their first calves, they are booted back to the 350,000-acre open range, where they stay until becoming aged cull cows.

At the end, the manager told us, as we look back at all the irrigated land, that "When the mine plays out in about twenty-five years, this will all return to a desert like the rest of the land around here."

No mine, so no water being pumped out.

Elko was our stop for the night. While I lost my usual twenty-five dollars, we did have a couple of folks pay for their trip at the casino. Early the next morning, after photo ops across the Bonneville Salt Flats, there was an afternoon flight home.

I should have ceased being a tour guide right then. Even though we have had a couple to rival this tour, we never again topped this one for interest and being inexpensive.

HIGHLIGHTS

Beginning this part, I mentioned that I would have some short blurbs about some of the best trips we have made. It would truly be way too much to highlight every tour. So here it goes. While I would like to tell some of the funny stories about people and happenings, I feel that, once I got started, I couldn't protect the guilty—maybe in an addendum. In addition, I could list lots of very helpful and memorable people, but am afraid that someone would be left out.

Best Meals (Keep the Important Stuff First)

We have eaten a lot of good food, and most of us gain weight while traveling, but in addition to a couple places mentioned earlier, here are my top five lists:

- Crawfish étouffée cooked by a rice farmer's wife in Evangeline Parrish, Louisiana
- Steaks at the Golden Ox in Kansas City
- Pizza at Pace's in Jamestown, New York
- Seafood feast prepared for us in Plaquemines Parrish, Louisiana
- Tri Tips and wine at Oak Ridge Ranch in California

Scenic Drives

- Across the Bighorn Mountains
- Yosemite N P
- Icefield Parkway north of Banff, Alberta
- Desert of Arizona
- Skyline Drive of Virginia in fall
- Columbia River Valley

Unusual Visits

- Forest fire in the Big Hole of Montana when we visited Sitz Ranch
- Largest Shitake mushroom grower in North America

- Three million bird duck farm
- Best Little Whorehouse in Texas (it joined a ranch we visited)
- Chili Pepper drying plant in New Mexico (cleared our sinuses)

One of the things that has happened over twenty-six years is that the cattle association tours and my personal travels have become complimentary. Whenever I am on a cattle tour, I always keep my eyes open for places and people to visit with my family and similarly do the same for cattlemen tours when on a personal trip. This has allowed both to become better.

ADVENTURES WITH ASHLEY

Grandchildren are one of God's greatest gifts (most of the time). Our first grandchild, Ashley, has proven to be just what a little girl should be, both a joy and sometimes a problem. I was raised in a family with nothing but boys and had all boys as children—all boys until I acquired two wonderful daughters by marrying Diane. However, they were not *little girls*. That first experience was reserved for our Ashley, to be followed by four more little girls. Have you ever noticed how granddaughters can get grandfathers to do just about anything they want them to do?

While we now have eight grandchildren, Ashley got there first, and is still the one that seems to be most interested in travels with G papa and G mama. But there is hope for the future that others will follow in her footsteps.

In 1997 when Ashley had just turned nine, we asked if she would like to go with us on a camping trip to Canada. She said sure she would try it. So off we went north. The first night was spent in a conservation area near Rondeau Provincial Park, as the park campground was full. Ashley, at this point, did not yet know the routine of getting set up quickly, so it was lesson time. The campground wasn't particularly great, but it was okay.

ASHLEY ON THE FIRST NIGHT OF
HER FIRST CAMPING TRIP

After a quick supper, a light drizzle started to fall, along with a cool wind. At that point, Ashley was starting to have second thoughts about camping, but we survived the night (not without some whining and a little homesickness) and woke to a cool, crisp morning. We had by then bought a slightly larger, three-person Kelty tent that we shared with her, so there was real togetherness.

After an early morning walk along Lake Eire, I found that rock collecting is definitely genetic. She also became extremely excited when she found *the snake* that turned out to be a stick, but certainly looked like a snake lying in the weeds at the edge of the water. Even now it is sitting just above me at the computer, peaking its head around the corner on top of a cabinet.

We followed the Lake Erie shore toward Niagara Falls. We stopped for lunch at the city park in Delhi, which is a really nice, small rural town. Whenever in the area, we almost always stop for at least a short visit with Mike Columbus, who is a crop specialist for the Ontario Ministry of Agriculture.

I became acquainted with Mike quite by accident. In setting up a tour for our cattle association, one of the people I knew from the cattle business suggested he would be great to help set up farm visits. Mike's official title is new crop specialist. At one time, Ontario was a major tobacco producer, but when the social pressure and taxes were increased the crop's importance declined. It fell to Mike to find and help develop some alternatives to help maintain farm income. He has been very successful in finding new crops that adapted to their environment. Kentucky was just starting to really feel the pressure on tobacco, so he was a natural for a visit.

He indeed proved to be a good contact that was proud of his work and had a lot of information to share. While there is not a lot of what they are doing that would be directly applicable to Kentucky, the process of finding, growing, and marketing is exactly the same. He helped develop an expanded greenhouse industry and worked to introduce new crops, such as sweet potatoes and peanuts, along with an already growing ginseng industry. We have used his help on three tours over the years, and I have stayed in contact and always enjoy a visit with him.

After lunch it was a short journey to set up camp at the same conservation area where we had camped with our son Charles a couple of years before near Welland. Then we were off to see Niagara Falls. Ashley was almost over-whelmed. The awe on her face alone would have made the whole trip worthwhile by itself. She was particularly impressed when we went through the tunnels to see the falls from below. We went back to camp, and then it was time for a swim before a late supper. By now she was sold on traveling and camping with little thoughts about missing home.

One of the interesting things about camping can be the people you meet. Camped next to us was a dairy farmer whose family set up their tent camper for a few weeks in the summer. He would commute back each morning to take care of the day's chores, while the family enjoyed the swimming, boating, and hiking. His dad would do the evening milking, so there was family time for him as well. He had sold several top-end Holstein show cows to herds in

Kentucky that I was acquainted with from helping with shows at the state fair.

The next morning it was an early start to get through Toronto on Sunday morning and beat any traffic. I usually avoid Toronto, because it is a miserable place for me to try and drive through. By mid-afternoon we reached our goal for the day, Fitzroy Provincial Park, where we planned to spend at least two nights. We had arrived with plenty of time for a short canoe on the Ottawa River, followed by a swim at the beach. By now Ashley was starting to get the camping thing pretty well down pat. Luckily, we reserved the campsite with the small waterfall on Carp River that runs through the park. That night we fixed one of Ashley's favorite meals—barbeque pork chops.

ASHLEY LOVES BARBEQUE PORK CHOPS

The park has a Sunday evening music event during the summer. That night the show featured Gail Galwin, a local TV personality that specialized in Irish music and dancing. It was all we could do to keep Ashley off the stage (we actually weren't successful). Guess that was shades of things to come as Ashley has become a pretty good dancer and is a budding diva, soon to start her third year in college as a vocal major in opera. Since writing this section, Ashley has become much more than a budding diva. Now a senior in college, she was named the outstanding vocal major at the University of Kentucky and has a leading role in their fall opera.

Ottawa was on the agenda for the next day, and we took in many of the things we had on previous visits. Only this time we were seeing it through new young eyes. Taking someone to visit and see places for the first time remains one of my favorite things to do. It is almost like I am seeing or doing it for the first time again. That night we had great grilled salmon.

After another day of R&R in and around Fitzroy, we headed back toward the United States. As always, we look for different routes rather than just follow the same ways we have before. This time, with a mid-morning start, we cut across southern Quebec to Sherbrooke (there were no problems this time and we didn't stop) and followed Route 212 to cross in to the United States at Coburn Gore. After a very relaxing and slow drive through the woods of northern Maine on Route 27, we swung a little west to camp at Mt Blue State Park. Diane's notes said it was cool and beautiful, but there were only pit toilets and no showers.

Since we had showered before we left Fitzroy it was all right for one night.

Our next stop was Camden Hills State Park on the coast of Maine. The weather was great, and like before we rode the sloop Appledore for a short cruise that afternoon. The only difference was that after clearing the harbor, they let Ashley steer. What a thrill for a nine year old.

ASHLEY IN CHARGE

Again that night we had visits from a raccoon, but not the big silverback from before. Camping with Ashley, we had to keep a constant eye out, as she was fearless when it came to animals, even though we kept telling her of the danger. I am just glad there weren't any bears around!

After another day of cruising on the Maine Ferries with a lobster supper and campfire, Ashley was all set for another first. Late the next afternoon she wanted to get in the ocean. We knew that Ashley wasn't bothered by cold water, but didn't think that in the very cold water along Maine's coast she would last very long, but she did. It made us cold just to watch her.

It was about time to head home, so with a leisurely start we headed west. That day we avoided any interstates as we wandered through southern New Hampshire, Vermont, south in western Massachusetts, and west and south again in New York. With that route we passed through such places as Keene, New Hampshire, North Adams, Massachusetts, and Ghent, New York, ending up in the Blackhead Mountains on the north side of the Catskills. It was not much of a route for covering miles quickly, but its great, relaxed driving and good for seeing the northeastern countryside.

Diane and I had eaten at the Point Lookout Mountain Inn a couple of times when leaving either my brother Jim in Massachusetts or my friend John in Rhode Island. We planned at some point to stay a night there. When we passed, it had always been either fairly early morning or lunchtime as we went that way. This route using Highway 23 to cross over north of New York City offers a couple of advantages. It is much easier driving, and it's a little shorter way to pick up Route 17 west, plus it's a lot more scenic. For the most part, you can move on pretty well with just enough small towns to make it interesting.

We decided to spend the night at the Inn, rather than set up at a campground—our first civilization on the trip. Point Lookout Mountain Inn has pretty good food and a super view. Like Lookout Mountain near Chattanooga, Tennessee, you can see several states and mountain ranges, including the Green, White, and Adirondacks on a clear day. The hotel itself is overpriced for the amenities, but almost worth the price just for the view. We hadn't realized that their main season was winter skiing, so that night there were only two rooms occupied, and the innkeeper left, just giving us a number to call if we needed anything.

The next morning made the stay worth it. It often takes a stick of dynamite to get Ashley awake and going in the morning, but not that day. With the weather clear and beautiful, we had half-jokingly told her to wake us up to see the sunrise. I have never needed an alarm clock and am an early riser, but I didn't beat Ashley up that morning.

Just as false dawn was creeping in, there she was bouncing on the bed with, "Wake up, Grandpapa. Let's see the sunrise."

Diane and I were completely shocked, but did sit with her on the deck and watch the sun come up. Both the sunrise and that morning with her are beautiful memories.

Route 17 is a pretty good drive for an interstate. Wandering across southern New York, it is not terribly crowded except around the cities. It winds through a mix of farmland and rolling hills, ending up at the Pennsylvania border just west of Jamestown, New York. That night we stayed at Geneva State Park, Ohio, on Lake Eire. Again, Ashley thrived in the cool northern waters. Guess I am either a wimp or too much of a southerner to enjoy swimming in cold water, but I am not young either. It was that night that we came the closest to a disaster with fearless Ashley.

Earlier I mentioned how fearless Ashley was around animals. Geneva State Park has skunks, rather than coons, as camp moochers. Usually, if you just ignore them, don't leave food out, and give them space, they are pretty well behaved. This night one wandered over toward our camp not too long before dark. I just about had to hogtie Ashley to keep her from approaching this seemingly tame critter. I think she understood, but just was hardheaded enough to try and find out for herself.

"It's so cute!" she insisted.

Just thinking I had this settled, there she is tossing cookies to attract the skunk closer.

"Enough!"

Off to bed with protest she went. Sure enough, not too much later the air is filled with eau de skunk from a campsite about 250 feet away. They found out that its best to leave even a campground moocher skunk alone.

The next day it was hard to head home from what had been a wonderful experience, not just for her, but for us as well. Many of the trips I have written about have been both a first and a last. This was different. Since that first adventure with Ashley, there have been many more. In writing this story, I have tried to recall them all, and best I can figure, she has accompanied us on at least fifteen trips since that first. Like the cattle association tours, I won't even try to describe them all, but will just hit a few highlights and one more very memorable trip.

Starting in 1998 Ashley went with us to the Apalachicola, Florida, area to camp. She went a couple of years by herself, then with her younger brother, Taylor, along. And two times we rented a beach house with her family and our youngest daughter's family. We had a great four-day weekend in Washington DC with her and her brother when I found almost unbelievably low airfares. That was a first flight for both of them.

A very memorable short trip was to Chicago for a sweet sixteen birthday present. We stayed in the most expensive suite I ever have stayed in. Ashley, her friend Laura, and G-mama shopped until they dropped. The most fun was had when we took in a musical version of Romeo and Juliet at the Shakespeare Theater. Our seats in that small venue were actually right on stage. There is one more detailed trip I want to tell before ending this section on "Adventures with Ashley." The summer she had just turned twelve we again headed to the northeast and up in to Canada to camp. This time, rather than straight north to cross in to Canada, we headed east to make a visit with my friend John in Rhode Island and his wife, Ellen. Only John wasn't in Rhode Island, but up on Lake Winnipesaukee in New Hampshire.

Our plan was to spend a couple of nights with Ellen, go on a whale watch on the Grand Banks, then spend another two to three days with John at the cabin on the lake. After that we headed up into Ontario and then home. Our first night we camped at Caledonia State Park just east of Chambersburg, Pennsylvania, which made the next day a fairly easy drive to Charlestown, Rhode Island.

Our favorite route, when not just driving back roads, has been to head north to pick up I-84 to just east of Danbury, Connecticut, and take Route 34 along the Housatonte River down to either I-95 or US 1. This isn't necessarily the shortest or quickest drive, but there is not much difference in time. And by not taking the shortest, usually most crowded routes, I end the day not nearly as worn-out from the constant road stress.

The two days in Rhode Island were great, and Ashley and Ellen hit it off right away. While she and John have no children, Ellen has spent a lot of volunteer time working with the Rainbow Girls. That afternoon was a trip to the beach, and the next day we visited the Mystic Seaport. Evenings were an experience. As I said, my experience had been exclusively male, so social interaction with a twelve-year-old girl, a rainbow leader, and Diane, a former rainbow girl, was all new to me. Maybe I even touched my feminine side (just a little). They managed to involve me in trying on old hats and wigs, which at least *they* found funny.

No comment!

Following two wonderful days, we left before daylight to take a morning whale watch out of Plymouth, Massachusetts. While Diane and I had been on a few previously, we got to see them again with young first-time eyes. Perched on the bow of the boat, Ashley got to see several humpbacks, plus other types of whales, some really up close.

Arriving back in port at eleven-thirty in the morning, we headed north to join John that afternoon on Lake Winnipesaukee in central New Hampshire. John's cabin was on an island in the middle of the lake. His grandfather had purchased five acres of the thirty-acre island in the late 1800s and built the first one-room cabin. It had become an annual summer event for his family to spend lots of time there. The cabin had been added to over the years to accommodate an expanded family and then grew smaller as the family decreased. The site was unusual in that it actually had a small beach. Electricity only became available a couple of years before we visited, and the only way to get there was by boat. John had spent weeks each summer there since he was a young boy. He was the last of his family to still use it as a summer vacation place. Today, few people want to spend most of a summer someplace where the most exciting thing is a daily visit from the post office boat that also has ice cream.

JOHN AND I SWAP LIES IN HIS CABIN

We met John at the mainland dock and boarded his eighteen-footer for a half-hour ride to our home for the next three nights. What an experience for Ashley to stay in a place where water comes from a pump, and the bathroom is a path to a little building with a crescent on the door. Bats flew everywhere in pursuit of the mosquitoes and night bugs. That first night I thought we might have to leave earlier than planned when a bat, after finding a small opening, flew around our bedroom searching for prey. During the winter, the bats hibernated in a space in the attic, which resulted in an ongoing problem. Raccoons thought the sleeping bats were just in cold storage for winter feast and often tore roofing and siding off to satisfy an acquired taste for fresh bat. John was in the process of roof repairs while we were there.

You would think that a twelve-year-old girl would be bored to tears in such a situation, but if she was it wasn't apparent. There was an old dory she learned to row around, found a place to swim and even had an island to explore with critters to find. Even though Ashley has traveled with us as she has grown into young womanhood, it seems that she enjoys just being a little girl again at times.

Maybe Ashley wasn't bored, and I really never recall actually being bored. Diane was quite content to sit, nap, and read in a lounge chair on the porch. However, I have never been able to just sit during the day even while involved in a good book. If it's daytime I have a great urge to be doing something, especially something useful. My type A personality has cooled as I have grown older, but it lurks just below the surface.

This is another way in which John and I have been almost opposites, so much so it's a wonder we have become fast friends. He is content to just seemingly piddle along, while I am a slasher and a banger. In the end, I finish a project first, but he is just shortly behind. Then after he has finished, with everything done exactly right, I am still going back to correct mistakes. I really wanted to jump in and get the roof repaired, but John just didn't want to get to it right then. Actually, in hindsight I think that if it got finished he felt he would then have to return south to the real world. He finished just as summer was winding down. So after three days we loaded back in the boat to head on our way. I won't cover ground previously traveled, but we had another good visit with our neighbors to the north in Canada.

The adventures with Ashley have continued, even as she has gone on to college. Every year since that first year, we have again continued our adventures. I know deep down that all good things come to an end, and whether last time was the last time or not, it has truly been an adventure. When Diane and I reflect on these good times, we will always be grateful for this opportunity. The mature, beautiful young lady Ashley is becoming is certainly a reflection of her parents' love and care, but we have been able to enrich her life experiences. She has done and tried many things that she would not have without us.

ASHLEY ALL GROWN UP

The travels with my children and grandchildren has enabled me to almost recapture that feeling of seeing or doing something for the first time. Maybe it is a little strange way of thinking, but in some little way the travels with my children or grandchildren gives me a small measure of immortality. I recall and retell stories my father told me about riding horseback with his grandfather around southwest Virginia in the early 1900s to buy livestock. And often he told of he and his father, even though living deep in the mountains of Pike County, Kentucky, catching a train to Chicago for what amounted to a long weekend. They would leave Friday and arrive for a White Sox game on Saturday and doubleheader on Sunday. They would get back on the train, returning home early Monday morning.

It hit me when on a trip that it is highly likely that stories of travels or doing things with their grandparents will likely be told to my great grandchildren. And if I get it written down, it may survive several generations into the future.

TRANSITIONS

There was one longer trip just with Ashley by herself, which was another time to Canada. After that, her younger brother Taylor started to go with us as well. And later her entire family made trips with us. The long weekend trip to Washington DC was his first, and then he also went camping two years in Canada.

There was an attempt to camp with Ashley, Taylor and their Mom and Dad that was only partially successful. Mindy and Lowell put up a brave front about camping, but it was evident that they never really got into it the way the kids and we had. They really enjoyed the seeing and doing, but would have preferred to have the more modern amenities of a motel for the nighttime. So in 2003 and 2004 it was back to camping with the kids during the summer.

During this time, Diane and I made several of what I call side trips, which were actually extended holiday weekends during the school year. There was our annual Labor Day trek someplace. Once we went to Gloucester, Massachusetts, which I have written a side story about and visited a few times. Another side trip was when we went to spend the weekend with my friend John and his wife, Ellen, in Rhode Island. It was on this trip that we first got to cruise Newport Harbor and Narragansett Bay.

I have described before that John was raised almost a waterman on Jamestown Island, and while he no longer lives there, he still has many ties to that beautiful, small community. His cousin bought a large lot that joined John's home place and established his family there. Matt Jamison's career was at first as a marine mechanic and now he has developed into a marine appraiser working for insurance companies and boat buyers. He has a small cruiser at the harbor less than a block from the home place. John convinced him to take a day cruise to see all the sites from the water. This ended up being one of the most enjoyable days we have ever spent with great people and good food.

It was during this period that we took our fall break trip to San Francisco, described earlier, and took another trip to see our son Nathan and our grandson in North Platte, Nebraska. During that visit, the large flocks of Sand Hills cranes and even some Whopping cranes along the Platte River awed us. We continued to take opportunities as they arose to see and do what we could afford.

SOMETHING DIFFERENT

In 2002 Diane and I made another journey to Canada that was a little outside the box. By now I was getting pretty good on the web, and chatting was fairly popular. I visited several chat rooms that were primarily farm chats and got introduced to what became my favorite room by a person I chatted with in one of them. A dairy farmer's wife from Ontario suggested that I try a room called Northern Lights. Even though it was listed as a romance room, in the early mornings it actually was like a coffee club gathering at a local watering hole. For me it was an escape from reality for a few minutes in the early morning.

The morning coffee club was an eclectic group. You could almost set your watch by the time they came and went from the room. Some of the varied people were: an apple farmer in New Zealand, a baker in British Columbia, a graduate student in Germany, a teacher at the embassy school in Beijing, a mayor in the Philippines, a photo journalist in Tibet, and of course a real diversity from eastern Canada. In the evening it was totally different, as it evolved in to a typical chat room by late afternoon, which I went into only a couple of times and that was enough.

One of the things they did start while I was still actively chatting was a summer gathering of those that frequented the room. I talked with them about the numerous times I had camped in Ontario, so they asked that I schedule a trip that coincided with their party. I thought it would be kind of neat to meet some of the people I had been talking with anonymously.

So it was that in late June of 2002 Diane and I set up camp in Confederation Park at Hamilton and attended the gathering. We didn't immediately join the group at the restaurant/nightclub where it was to be held. Sitting on a small deck adjacent to the party area, it was so strange that even though I had never met any of the people I was able to put faces with chat handles for many of them.

I had experiences with Canadians and partying before. The Canadian cattle herds would often bring show cattle to the United States, and we had exhibited cattle at the Canadian Royal in Toronto. A tradition is for those with the show champion to put on a celebration with libations for the rest of the exhibitors in the show. Well, this group from the chat room was not showing cattle, but they did know how to party. I like to think it was old age, but there was no way I could keep up with them, even if I had been younger. By the way, the campground at Confederation Park was actually pretty nice and well laid-out for an in-town campsite. It was clean, with good site separation and facilities. The only drawback was its closeness to a major road that could be noisy.

There was one couple, Del & Len, that I became friends with on the Internet. She was a nurse in a small town fairly close to where we liked to camp at Fitzroy Provincial Park, and, like me, never took seriously what was said in the chat room and liked to come up with zingers. Del also used the chat room as a short escape for a few minutes of frivolity before heading out to a high stress job.

The next couple of times we visited in Canada we would stop for a visit with Del and Len. They would also join us for an afternoon at Fitzroy. The grandkids really thought they were lots of fun to visit with and that it was neat to get to meet people from another country. As I have said, the people you meet add to the fabric of life.

LIFELINE UPDATE

In August of 2002 I reached the sixty-year-old milestone and had enough years to retire. It was time for a change. After so long I had enough of going to night meetings, being on call almost twenty-four/seven, and having a demanding schedule. I like to tell the truth, and the first thing I did driving home on my last workday was to be a litterbug. As soon as I got on the road home I pitched my schedule book out the window, and to this day I refuse to carry another one.

Even though I was retiring, it didn't mean I was not going to work. I will quit working when I can no longer physically or mentally do something productive. It was my intention to be pretty much fully employed, except on my own terms and schedule.

For a couple of years before retiring, we had been expanding our registered Angus cowherd and starting to grow crops for the farmers market. We had leased a larger farm to facilitate the expansion. Another thing that I also really wanted to do was start working at Keeneland Race Track during the race meets. I was raised with horses, even owned a racehorse, and knew many who worked at the track. Finally, I planned to do some substitute teaching when the mood or weather suited me. I slowed down, but still kept chugging along.

Until 2007 the cowherd did really well. Our drought in 2007 and 2008 put a damper on any more expansion, and we have actually cutback a few cows because of the feed short-age. For the first four years, I grew from five to seven acres of vegetables to sell; however, with a lot of renovation needed on our house, I didn't grow any in 2007 and 2008. It's a good thing, as the drought would have almost made it impossible to make any money on vegetables.

My job at Keeneland turned out better than I ever hoped. I would have been content to do about anything, no matter how menial it appeared. Sometimes you are lucky. Just a few days after dropping off a job application, I got a call. How would you like to be a horsemen's bookkeeper? The current bookkeeper was taking a full time job elsewhere.

ABOUT KEENELAND

Keeneland is unique in the horse racing industry. It was founded in the 1930s by a group of local horsemen and was set up as a non-profit organization that would promote our horse industry. Any profits must go to facility improvements or to charity. Keeneland has become a major charitable contributor in Kentucky, and racing is very successful. While it is not always true, we now have some of the highest average purse-money in the world. Each year many of the top racehorses from around the world come to Keeneland to run. And while not as famous amongst the general public as Churchill Downs and the Kentucky Derby, Keeneland is where horsemen really like to race their horses.

While racing does make some money for the association, the big income producer is horse sales. Central Kentucky sells more dollars' worth of horses than the rest of the world combined. Breeders and racehorse owners come from all over the world to the Keeneland sales.

From the average race fan's point of view, this isn't what makes Keeneland special. We do racing the way it should be. The grounds are clean and beautifully landscaped, and unlike many tracks it has been a policy to be a family-friendly place.

My job allows me to get there early for the morning workout time, and each morning there are families, mothers with young children, and some school groups that visit. On Saturday mornings we *have Breakfast at the Works*, which has a very reasonable breakfast buffet with demonstrations and programs that are just for kids. It is not unusual to have thousands attend.

A couple of years ago, when the horse Smarty Jones was training for the Derby, I overheard his trainer talking on the phone to the owner, "They have more people here to watch the morning workouts than we do on our race days at home," he commented.

Even during the afternoon races, families are very evident. Right next to my office is an open grass area just past the finish line that is populated by families there to enjoy a day of racing. It is a Kentucky tradition. I remember my parents taking me at an early age, and I remember skipping out of high school to go to the races, only to find several of my teachers had the same idea. Even if you are not a horserace fan, a visit to Keeneland for the race meets is well worth your time.

Most of my year is spent working alone on the farm or around the house, so I believe the part-time jobs keep my mind sharper. But those weeks are enough to be regulated. The other thing that the part-time work provides is some extra discretionary spending money that has paid for several trips

Even though retired, I still have a fairly full-time work schedule. I especially, except for the Keeneland weeks, try to build in at least thirty to thirty-five hours of physical work each week. So for eight years I have been retired, but not really retired

BEACH WEEKS

Twice we rented a beach house during spring breaks—the first time we packed up our oldest daughter, Mindy, along with Ashley and Taylor. We were going back to Cape San Blas near Apalachicola, Florida, again. Mindy had made the trip up to see her grandparents in Poquoson, Virginia, that was just a long weekend, so I had never spent a longer period with her, just the kids. This proved to be a really enjoyable week. In 2004 we expanded the bunch going for spring break. In addition to Mindy and the kids, we added her husband, Lowell.

We ate great, and I didn't have to do all the cooking. A full sack of oysters, pounds of fresh caught shrimp, and some big grouper filets all added to our seafood feasts. On our first trip down camping with Ashley, we discovered that she didn't need to acquire a taste for fresh oysters on the half shell—she already had it. Along with Diane and I, she could about eat her weight in them, raw or grilled. Like daughter, like mother. Mindy too could really work on them. However, we didn't have to share with Lowell and Taylor, so there was more for us. This time down, we had the best luck surf-fishing of any time I had been there. We caught so many that it almost became tiring.

We returned to Cape San Blas in the next year with a full house of twelve. Mindy and family, plus two friends, had rented a minivan and were leaving the day after we left. Diane and I, along with Missy and the girls, would leave and stop for the night in Alabama, then arrive late morning at our rental house. While we ended up having a great time on the beach, it was the trip down that made this journey so memorable.

Missy has twin daughters (Savannah and Mackenzie) who were eight at the time. Even though we had never traveled with them, they had spent quite a lot of time with us. The youngest daughter, Madeline, had just turned two in December. You need to know that Maddy (aka mad Maddy) somewhat resembled my state of mind in my younger days. After all, she was two and the baby. The major difference is that she is actually very funny and knows it. Traveling with a two-year-old on a long drive offers all kinds of potential for a miserable trip.

The first thing to happen was on the shortcut I took to reach the Bluegrass Parkway west. It would save almost fifteen miles. However, there are some twists and turns. Halfway across, I heard a *urrrpp*. We found out what Maddy had for breakfast. Although not prone to carsickness, she was that morning. Everything settled down by the time we hit the parkway with me driving 25 mph the rest of the way on the side road.

We went right on through Nashville and made a stop for lunch with all going real well and were on schedule to make a fairly early stop for the night in Troy, Alabama. At this point in time Maddy was just about finished with toilet training. In order to facilitate this, we bought a brand new *Dora Let's Go Potty* seat. It didn't take long for her to realize that when she said she had to go to potty, not only would we stop, but she got to use her *Dora* and run around. In spite of this, we were still rolling along and passed through Birmingham, Alabama, about two in the afternoon, which would put us to Troy, Alabama, by about five in the evening before dark. We planned to stop at Troy for a couple of reasons. It was a fairly short morning drive on to Cape San Blas. However, the main reason was that on our previous trip down with Mindy and the kids, we had discovered a small non-descript strip-mall restaurant that served the best Buffalo Shrimp I have ever eaten (gluttony, anyone?).

South of Birmingham all the plans went down the drain. About halfway between two exits several miles apart we came to a screeching halt. Interstate 65 had become a parking lot. *Okay,* there was an accident ahead and it would clear before too long. When fifteen minutes later I finally got to the top of a rise, traffic stood in front of me for over a mile, all basically sitting still like me. To make it even worse, the dividing drain was too deep to try to crossover and go back to the last exit and then find another side road. I carry an emergency CB, so I finally got in touch with a northbound trucker. The accident was a semi with a hazardous load just north of Montgomery, and even one northbound lane was closed. To add to the traffic problems, US 31, which I could cut over to if I ever reached the next exit, was mobbed with traffic, and there was an accident on it too. The only other practical route would be to go west about twenty miles and pick up US 82 down to Montgomery.

For the next hour and forty-five minutes I was cooped up in a crew cab pickup with five females and one of them a two-year-old. It was not a particularly pleasant experience. In all honesty, they were really good and Maddy actually kept us cracked up. Fortunately, we had taken a potty break just shortly after we cleared Birmingham. Maddy, with two-year-old reasoning that saying potty would get her out of her car seat to run around, did consistently remind us that she needed to potty. By that time, she was saying she needed to *Dora*.

Finally, we reached the next exit, having covered three and a half miles in two hours. Whew, we were finally rolling and quickly found that potty stop. We reached the south side of Montgomery at six-thirty in the evening. There was no buffalo shrimp that night. We stopped at a Frisch's for plain, chain restaurant food. Maddy, having become tired of us as her all-day company, proceeded to work the crowd and even entertain the Big Boy clown, who was making a guest appearance that evening.

It was almost nine when we finally reached our motel in Troy, which was a little over four hours after we planned to arrive—an interesting day that was over eleven hours long rather than about eight. Sometimes major disruptions can make a trip memorable. In spite of the great time at the beach and super seafood, it was the long day with a two-year-old, who kept needing to *Dora,* that really sticks in my mind and always brings a smile.

GETTING TO KNOW
MY DAUGHTER

I acquired Mindy as a daughter when Diane and I were married. Missy, our youngest daughter, was just finishing 8th grade when we hooked up and spent all of her high school years and college breaks with our home as her home. Mindy, on the other hand, was a senior in high school, as well as a dancer with the Lexington ballet, and chose (rightfully so) to finish school with her class that she had been with since elementary school and lived with her father several miles away that year. Yes, we spent some time and holidays together, but with college, marriage, and children, plus establishing a thriving dance studio, there was really little time to *bond*.

MINDY'S ORGANIZATION

I have to pause and tell one story about Mindy and college. She and her sister are almost complete opposites in many ways, each unique. Mindy is very liberal, whereas Missy is very conservative. In addition, in their younger years Missy was always a neat freak (and still is). Diane tells me that, even as a little girl, Missy would not even go to bed unless every toy and all of her things were exactly in its place. Mindy, on the other hand, believed in organized chaos. One look at her room and you would wonder how anything was ever found. But she could always go right to what she wanted, even if it seemed almost a miracle each time she did.

Nothing exemplifies this difference more than my experience moving each of them out of their dorm room when they finished their first year at college. The first time I went to help Missy move out everything was boxed, packed, and labeled. However, with Mindy it was another story. Arriving at the dorm, she wasn't even there. We were informed by her roommate that she was off on a picnic date and would be back after a while. Entering her room, it was no different than at home, looking like a tornado just passed through. Being a good mother, Diane brought some boxes and large trash bags (maybe she had an inkling of what we would find). After waiting a half-hour, it crosses my mind that the best strategy would be to back the pickup up under her second story window and pitch anything not breakable down to the truck bed in the bags. (And I came real close to doing just that.) Fortunately, Mindy finally showed up; she and Mom stuffed, and I carried. I still like to tease her about that day, even though her house in no way resembles that dorm room. (I don't look in hidden places.)

We started slow with the trip to see her grandparents, the two trips down to Cape San Blas, and the semi-successful camping trip to Canada. On these treks it became apparent that Mindy really enjoyed traveling and was always ready for a little different experience. Plus, she was a lot like her mother in that she could get excited about seeing or doing something small that may be missed by the average traveler. I really enjoyed travel with her, as I did with her daughter Ashley.

Almost all of her travel experiences had been getting in the car and riding straight through to spend the week at Myrtle Beach. Her children had seen much more of the wonders of our wonderful country than she had. As I said earlier in this story, it is my belief that anyone who has not really seen this nation along its highways and byways, not just a few highlights, is truly deprived.

With Mindy's children growing up and the fact we had enjoyed our limited travel together, Diane and I discussed that maybe we could get them to accompany us on a couple of trips. I had provided my sons with opportunities to travel, see, and do. As I told Mindy, it was time to start completing her education.

After our very great time with the bunch at Cape San Blas over spring break, we started discussing maybe making a summertime trip. However, we figured funds and schedules would make it hard to do. I had some places in mind, but nothing concrete.

CALIFORNIA OR BUST

Fate can change things in a heartbeat. In early June I was starting to plan another tour for the Cattle Association and was more watchful of airfares and travel deals than usual. Timing, using specials to negotiate with airlines, car rentals, etc. can often result in anything from a few dollars to several saved. For one person a ten-dollar savings isn't too important, but it can knock off hundreds with a group. Do that a couple of times and soon you are talking real money. A few years ago when booking vans for the cattle association we went through five sets of reservations before we traveled and ended up saving six hundred dollars for the group. If I had been getting paid, the savings represented over two hundred dollars per hour spent.

Any sleep specialist would question my sleep habits, but I make it somehow. Most of my life, I have rarely slept much more than six hours a night and often in at least two segments. Middle of the night awake-time is often used for reading, writing, and in later years, surfing the web.

Just on a whim to see how airfares to the west coast were running, I did a price request to the San Francisco area. I just about fell out of my chair. Who would have expected a round trip for $119 per person, including tax and fees? I immediately typed in the same request for six people. I booked it, and as soon in the morning as I dared, called Mindy and asked if they wanted to go to California.

"Huh? Sure! When?"

Luckily, I knew when her summer dance camps ended and when they planned to drive to the beach for a few days and had booked a time between the two. Also luckily for us, we had really good bull sales that spring and cash flow from the farmers market sales were up, so finances, which are never great for me, were better than normal. Diane and I had only planned to make a short camping trip that summer, but this was just too good to pass up.

As with most good deals, there is a catch twenty-two. The price only applied to a specific Saturday afternoon flight that got to San Francisco after midnight Pacific Time and the return had to be on the midnight redeye on Thursday night. Even more different was that even though I booked through USAir, the flights were on United. Aren't airlines strange sometimes? That was okay with me, because when I can find an affordable trip that runs just about a third of normal cost, I just about can't resist. This was the best deal I have ever found.

A Saturday morning of selling at the farmers market, a change of clothes, and we were off. By the time we arrived at SFO, I was bushed, so it's a good thing my son-in-law is a night person. It was four o'clock in the morning Eastern Time when we arrived at Jack London Inn in Oakland. On my biological clock, I slept late that morning. Eyes popped open at seven o'clock in the morning Pacific Time, after the usual six hours of sleep. The rest of the crew, however, required more sleep, and they usually start the day later than I would. I had breakfast at the Buttercup Restaurant up the street, which is frequented the local constabulary that time of day, took a walk around the marina, and had a visit with farmers setting up for their Sunday farmers market in Jack

London Square, and it was nine o'clock in the morning. It was time to rouse the troops.

The first thing on our agenda was to drive up to Skyline Drive along the crest of hills to the east. Diane and I had discovered this a few years before. If the weather is clear, there are vistas where you can see from San Rafael in the north to Palo Alto in the south. This was only the second time we found conditions clear enough to get the whole view. We went back down the hills for lunch and took a walk through the farmers market, and then we were off to see San Francisco. In addition to functioning well at night, Lowell loves to drive when traffic was like it is crossing the Bay Bridge. Lowell was in the proverbial hog heaven

With the longer day length in summer, we were able to squeeze a lot in that afternoon. We planned to take the ferry across the next morning and use public transportation to see much of what was on our priority list. Bypassing the waterfront part of the city, we went directly to the coast and Golden Gate Park for a visit to observe how San Franciscans spent Sunday in the park, and we visited the Japanese Tea Garden. Leaving the park, we were heading for Golden Gate Bridge. At a stoplight on our way, a large African American man called over to me from his car and asked if this was the way to the bridge.

There is no doubt that the Golden Gate Bridge is one of the premier manmade landmarks in America. Having watched the story of building it on the Discovery Channel, it is an engineering marvel. This day it was clear with little fog. Several times when I've visited much of the bridge and the view of San Francisco has been obscured by the fog rolling in from the Pacific. We did our photo op and *ooed and awed* about the bridge.

ALL OF US AT THE GOLDEN GATE BRIDGE

Then it was up to the Marin Headlands to look back at both the bridge and bay from a different angle. By then my internal clock was saying *supper time is past,* so it was back to Oakland for a great meal at Il Pescatore, which is a really good place to eat and has a mix of seafood and Italian.

Monday morning we joined the commuters on the Oakland Alameda Ferry. Riding the ferries around San Francisco Bay is a great way to get some different views and a cheap way to get around. For my fellow travelers it was their first time to see a large port facility up close as we headed toward San Francisco.

CALIFORNIA STRANGE
AND SERENDIPITY

While waiting for the ferry that morning, a large black man accompanied by a beautiful young lady came up to also board the ferry.

Not being shy and often speaking to strangers, I said, "Hi."

He greeted me back.

Taking a good look at him, he looked familiar. Again, not being shy talking to strangers, I asked where I might have seen him before.

After some exchanges, we came up with it. He was the fellow asking about Golden Gate Bridge the day before. And it gets stranger. Seeing my University of Kentucky cap, he asked where I was from. Turns out he is originally from Louisville, Kentucky, and played basketball at a local high school there and then at San Diego State. His cousin was Darrel Griffin, an all-American at the University of Louisville, and we knew several people in common. That day, as we toured, we ran into each other at least five times.

Again, while waiting for the ferry, we were approached by a Chinese lady about our age. She saw we were traveling as a family and felt comfortable talking to us in her broken English. She wanted to know where we were going. It seems that she and her husband were fairly recent immigrants from Taiwan; they were participating in a tutoring program that would help them both with their English and assimilating in to US culture. Her problem was that their tutor had not shown up yet, and they were worried they would get off at the wrong stop. Her husband was a retired dentist, and their son was already a US citizen finishing medical school. We assured her we would make sure that they found where they wanted to go.

While on the ride across the bay, Diane, the lady, and her husband had a long conversation. It turned out that the husband handled English better than his wife.

During that conversation, Diane, who loves Chinese food, asked, "Have you been here long enough to pick out a really good, authentic Chinese restaurant?"

He proceeded to say they had.

The only problem was he couldn't tell us the name in English, but it was on Kearney Street, and you could see the Chinatown Holiday Inn from it. He did say he could write the name down for us though. The only paper Diane had was a deposit slip from her checkbook, and he wrote the name down, along with the name of a restaurant in Oakland. However, it was written in Chinese, and not wanting to embarrass him, she thanked him for the help.

Later in the day, we went to Chinatown and to the area of Kearney Street, where you could see the Holiday Inn. It was there that Dennis's lack of shyness in talking to strangers came through. It wasn't until I had asked six people when I found a Chinese-appearing person who could actually read Chinese. We found the restaurant. It may not be the best or most authentic, but we were the only people who were not Asian in the place, and the food was great. Wish I could tell you the name, but I never found out what its English equivalent was either. However, I do tell people that I can take them to the best Chinese restaurant in San Francisco's Chinatown, just for an opportunity to tell this story.

As we passed under the Bay Bridge and headed toward the Ferry Terminal stop, something really hit me for the first time. I knew that it was always personally rewarding for me to show people places and do things with them for their first time, but during that ride it became crystallized in my mind.

Watching our daughter, Lowell, and especially Ashley and Taylor, I told Diane, "You know we are building memories that will outlive us for a long time. Can't you just see Ashley or Taylor visiting here with their grandchildren and telling them about a visit with their Gpapa and Gmama a long time ago?"

Like life, the journey is most rewarding by what happens along the way.

Arriving at Pier 39, we proceeded to do the tourist thing so many people have in San Francisco—Fisherman's Wharf, cable cars, trolleys, Chinatown, and more. Even though we have visited the area several times and seen quite a bit, there is no doubt that we have merely scratched the surface. It could take weeks to actually say that you had seen San Francisco. In spite of my aversion to spending longer blocks of time in a city, in small doses I do enjoy visiting, with people watching being a major attraction. And certainly in San Francisco you can become a rubberneck trying to take in the huge diversity of its people.

Back in Oakland, we went to a great, small seafood restaurant south of downtown. It's unusual that I do not remember the name of a place with good food at a reasonable price and even worse when I was out there last fall and just couldn't find it. It was recommended to us by one of the hotel staff as someplace mostly patronized by locals. I guess I will have to go back again and do a more thorough search.

On Tuesday morning, we were going to visit Muir Woods. If you don't see much else, Muir Woods is a must see in the Bay Area. In addition to Muir Woods, we had two more things on the agenda: we wanted to drive up Route 1 along the coast and then cut back over to the Napa Valley and make a visit to a winery.

As always, Muir Woods didn't disappoint. Just a slow quiet walk through the ancient giants, it is very much like a religious experience every time I go I experience it, and most people that I have taken have the same reaction. Following the walk in the woods, we headed north up the coast. A tip: if you or anybody with you has a tendency for carsickness, make sure that they have their Dramamine dose before starting to the woods or up the coast on Route 1.

Knowing we would just be making a leisurely drive with great vistas, and since it was a beautiful day, we packed a picnic lunch. We had fresh fruit, cheese, and sourdough bread at picturesque picnic grounds in Tomales Bay State Park. After a good break, we headed back inland.

I have visited wineries in several sections of the country. On cattle association tours we visited the Biltmore Estate Winery near Ashville, North Carolina, one at the Amana Colony in Iowa, another in the hill country north of San Antonio, and one near Jamestown, New York. Diane and I visited wineries both in the Finger Lakes of New York and in California. One of the things that struck me was the evolution of the winery tour. While most of our visits were stops along the way, touring wineries has become an activity and goal in itself. Originally, they were efforts to just sell wine to the visitors. However, now they are selling the winery tour activity as an agri-tourism income source. Our early visits never involved a fee to tour or even to taste the wine, but just last fall when visiting Twin Valley Winery near Healdsburg, California, there was a forty-dollar charge, and that was a discounted group rate. Many wineries now have extensive gardens and attractive visitor centers, along with special events throughout the year.

That afternoon we visited a winery, and I chose not to pay the fee and do the tour as it was not a new experience for me and not really worth the cost from my perspective. I prefer the free tour and tasting as a confirmed cheapskate. My fellow travelers, however, really enjoyed the experience, and I enjoyed the beautiful grounds and people watching. Back at Oakland we had another good meal on Jack London Square. There are several good places to eat around the square, not what I would call great, but they deliver a pretty good meal at reasonable prices for the Bay area.

Wednesday morning was our day to head inland. Heading east on I-580 in the morning, you are going opposite of all the commuter traffic, so driving is fairly easy. It's always amazing to me that you leave the cool of the Bay area and are so shortly in the heat of the inland valleys. One thing to plan on seeing if you head east are the windmill farms located on the mountains east of Oakland. It is quite a sight to see the hundred-foot blades turning in the early morning sun in order to provide some of the electricity to the heavily populated region just to the west. We headed on east via I-205 to pick up Route 120 toward Yosemite. If we had more time, we would have dropped down to Modesto before heading on east. Around Modesto there are a couple of places I like to visit. The Gallo Family has Vintage Angus Ranch there (if you have the right contacts),. and the Fiscalina Dairy Farm is also just outside the city. The Fiscalina Dairy is transitioning from selling just milk to establishing a specialty market for their own brand of cheese. Their cheddar was recently recognized as the top English-style cheddar in the world, making it the first US cheese to receive such an honor.

Before lunchtime we arrived in Yosemite Valley. I think one of the things that has recently made California a favorite place to visit is the fact that you can be on the cool, rugged coast, in the hot desert valley, and in high mountains in less than a half day. Yosemite has almost endless spectacular views of mountains, monoliths, and hanging waterfalls. Carved by the glaciers of the last ice age, it is unique in its topography.

That afternoon was devoted to seeing as much as possible in our limited timeframe. Like too many places, all you get is an overview without devoting days to exploring the nooks and crannies that hide so much worth experiencing. This was a visit that brought back good memories from many years in the past. On the tour that I had made with my parents before shipping out to Asia some forty-four years before, we had entered Yosemite over Tioga Pass in July with a fresh covering of over six inches of snow.

Our last stop was the Mariposa Grove of Giant Sequoias. Unlike the visit I had made with snow still surrounding the trees, this day had temperatures in the upper eighties. While most of the time I thrive at higher altitudes, between the heat and altitude I about pooped out hiking up the mountain to see the upslope big ones. What a difference forty years makes.

Our motel for the night was in Mariposa. The Mariposa Lodge is not a chain facility but locally owned and operated by the same family for nearly fifty years as an independent. If not the fanciest motel, it certainly was one the cleanest and best maintained places I remember staying in. The courtyard had a really great display of landscape plants, all of which were marked as to what they were. It's a motel I can recommend as a great value.

Before daylight on Thursday, we were off for a long day and night. Heading back southwest past Merced, Los Banos, and Hollister, we arrived in Monterey by ten-thirty in the morning. We had lunch on Fisherman's Wharf, and I had arranged for us to go on an afternoon whale watch. Diane, Ashley, and I went on a whale watch on the east coast, but we had never been out in the Pacific. Like the east coast, don't let the shore temperature influence your wardrobe for a whale watch. It's in the middle seventies on shore and lower fifties or less out on the ocean. We left at noon, and after traveling a few miles from shore *thar she blows*. A 105-foot blue whale was spotted, and even though Humpbacks are impressive, the blue is simply awesome.

On the way back in, I was viewed with wonder by my wife and family. Having already been a long day with more to come, I proceeded to curl up by the rear transom of the boat and get a nice nap in. They still don't understand how I can just lay down on a hard wooden deck on a tossing boat and cool breeze and blip out, but I can.

Back in Monterey we just cruised the downtown touristy part, did some souvenir shopping, and enjoyed people watching, as always. The only thing I look back and regret was not having enough time to visit the Aquarium, which is great. Later in the afternoon, we just had to make the Seventeen Mile Drive past Pebble Beach and see how really wealthy people's homes look. Lowell, the avid golfer in the family, even had a photo op at Pebble Beach Golf Course. Even though never in my future, I can hope that maybe a lottery win or inheritance from some long lost relative will provide enough funds to at least spend a week in one of the modern castles on that beautiful coast

Our flight home was scheduled to head out just after midnight, so around six in the evening we headed north up Route 1. This section of the coast highway is not as spectacular as either north of San Francisco or down the Big Sur, but I really like the drive. Passing artichoke, strawberry, and many other crops with interruptions of high bluffs along the ocean, makes it a diversified trip. We had been snacking all day and still had leftovers, so before sunset near Half Moon Bay, we found a place to watch the day end in the continental United States and picnic on a vista of the Pacific Ocean—a good way to end our tour.

We made it to the airport in plenty of time and boarded our redeye home. We changed planes at daylight in Chicago and were back to Louisville shortly before eleven in the morning. I can sleep on a plane when I want but usually don't, because I think I might miss something, but I did sleep this time. Diane just about never can sleep in that situation, so she was about spaced out, having been awake for over twenty-four hours when we landed. After we arrived home I made a quick change of clothes and headed to the field to pick vegetables for the next day's farmers market. By late afternoon I was ready for a cool one and a good night's sleep in my own bed.

Looking back on this trip, we had too short of a time and tried to see too much, but I would do it again in a heartbeat. Opportunities to really get to know and have great experiences with your children and grandchildren are all too often rare in today's world. We accumulated memories that are priceless.

ARIZONA ADVENTURE

The next year we had such a great time on spring break and the previous summer tour that over Christmas we started discussing doing something again the next year. It turned out that our daughter Missy's family was planning something over spring break by themselves, so it would be just Mindy's family and us. We came up with two options: we could go back to the beach at Cape San Blas or head to Arizona. Normally, my job at Keeneland Race Track overlaps spring break, but not this year. And my spring calving period would be finished by then.

The year before I had planned a tour for fifty-seven people for our cattle association to Montana and ran all the expenses through my credit card. Along with a bump voucher, I had enough freebees stored up for six round trips for us, but didn't want to use them all for spring so I could save some for a later adventure. Starting just after Christmas, I began looking for deals to Arizona. Most people just look for round trip on an airline, but every once in a while you can find great one way deals, and I have booked different airlines and even two different airports in the same area for outbound and return.

Diane and I did this a couple of years ago over fall break. Heading to the central coast of California, we flew in to Ontario and back from San Jose. And while I have only seen it a couple of times with car rental by returning the car at SJC rather than ONT, we actually saved eighty dollars on the rental.

I particularly like shopping Southwest, because fares are not dependent on a round trip but independent for each way. After having found the great fares the previous summer, I was confident that with persistence something good would show up. If not, we had the option to do the beach thing again over spring break.

In late January, success! Southwest ran a special from Louisville to Phoenix for fifty-nine dollars if we left on the early Saturday morning flight. However, return fares were higher. Booking the outbound flight at fifty-nine dollars, I used three rapid rewards (six one ways) for the return flight, which left three round trip rewards for later. The total round trip airfare cost was just over four hundred dollars including taxes for all six of us.

On Saturday morning we flew out of Louisville in the dark and made Phoenix at nine o'clock in the morning. I do like to start early and stop early! We gathered our luggage, got the minivan, and were on the road heading east on I-10 toward Tucson. A couple of years before our cattle association had visited Saguaro National Park while in Arizona, and I thought that would make a great first stop. That cattlemen's trip was the first time since the Beginnings trip that I had been in southern Arizona, even though I had been in the north part of the state several times. Saguaro National Park was to be our first real stop of the trip. It was after a long, cold, wet winter, and in the seventy-degree sunshine we could have just basked like a seal on a beach.

Saguaro National Park is a great introduction to the Sonora Desert. The environment, plants, and animals are explained within the visitor center. I particularly like the slide show that ends with the screen opening, and there it is, the desert with the large Saguaro cactus spread out in front of you. After learning about how long these cacti live, about their skeletons and how they are threatened by humans, we walked among them as well as many other varieties.

Nearby is the International Wildlife Museum that is a good stop to learn about the critters that inhabit this environment. The two things I remember most are the raptor flying demonstration and the hummingbird display. Diane is a huge fan of hummingbirds. With several species nesting and flying around us, I just about had to drag her out of the enclosure. It was, after all, past time for lunch.

After lunch, we headed for our motel. It quite often turns out that we use a chain motel; however, I always look first for a locally owned and operated place that is not part of a chain. It has been my experience that most often if they own and operate without a chain affiliation, it is either a dump or a great value. This time I found a great value. The Smugglers Inn on East Speedway is not the fanciest but is a lot more than adequate with a beautiful courtyard, pool, and large, clean rooms. The courtyard was particularly impressive to me, along with the service conscious staff.

A secondary reason for stopping in Tucson was for a visit with Diane's nephew, John DeViese, who is stationed at Davis Monthan Air Fort Base. He is an A-10 Warthog mechanic, who just finished a tour in Afghanistan and was on the road to marriage. At that time his mom hadn't met the prospective bride, so we had an assignment: check her out. We had a nice visit with them and toured the base and *bone yard,* which is where there are hundreds of mothballed airplanes. The planes range from waiting to be scrapped to needing a cleanup, checkup and fuel up, and they are back in the air. As he was on duty that weekend, there wasn't a lot of time together, but we had a nice visit nevertheless.

After an afternoon of relaxing and some pool time, we got to do one thing that I really wanted for us to do, which was find a fairly authentic Mexican style restaurant complete with Mariachi music. In recent years several decent local Mexican restaurants have established here, but those in the southwest are usually better. Searching the web turned up El Fuente. El Fuente is not much on exterior appearance and is located in an older part of downtown, but the décor inside is fine. Our meal ended up being really good, and the atmosphere was a lot of fun. A highlight was the fresh made Guacamole and the music. However, my son-in-law has a different opinion. As it was his night to buy, he thinks the one hundred dollar plus margarita bill may have skewed our judgment, even though he too thought the food was good.

His comment was, "The food bill was okay for a good restaurant, but the bar bill made it an expensive place to eat."

Early the next morning, it was off to visit Mexico at Nogales. Nogales is a typical border town with lots of *stuff* for sale; it's very crowded and not really like farther down in Mexico. Of all the towns along the border I have visited, my favorite was when Diane and I went across to Piedras Negras as the only Anglos on the bus and in the town early in the morning. This was a totally new experience for all of Mindy's family. We had a good time wandering the narrow streets and vendor stalls. There is even a classic picture of me, complete with a sombrero mounted on a donkey that is wearing my hat.

POOR DONKEY!

When we had our fill of shopping, it was time to fill our bellies. Crossing back across the border, we stopped at the McDonalds just inside the United States; same old fat-laden, greasy food that is typical of that chain. However, there was a difference; this one had live music and a nice outside sitting area.

Back at the Smugglers Inn we had another short visit with our nephew before he went on duty. He mentioned that, although touristy, Trail Dust Town had some decent places to eat. We did manage to have a good *flat iron steak*.

The flat iron steak is showing up more often now in our meat cases. This is actually a tender muscle taken out of what would have been a chuck roast. In recent years, researchers using cattlemen grower funds have developed several new beef cuts and products. The flat iron steak is becoming one of the more successful new cuts. One caution if you are grilling: this cut is very lean, and even slightly over cooking it can result in a dryer, tough steak. If you don't like it slightly pink, you probably won't like the flat iron steak.

We enjoyed our meal, but what we did later was a highlight. Leaving Trail Dust Town, we headed up toward Mount Lemon in the dark. Drive up that winding road and you will eventually end up near nine thousand feet. All along the way there are beautiful vistas with all of metro Tucson's lights spread out below.

The next morning at daylight, we made a start north for more adventures. After a photo op at Biosphere II, we wound up the valleys between the Tortilla and Mescal Mountains, stopping for lunch at Show Low. That afternoon was spent in a short exploration of Petrified Forest National Park and the Painted Desert. It came to mind that with the number of visitors, even in this off season time, that if each one took a small piece of petrified wood, there would be no Petrified Forest left. For all but me this was a completely new experience. Naturally, I was in my element, getting to be the travel guide and, more importantly, seeing it again with fresh eyes.

As we headed west for our night at Flagstaff, we had a fun stop. The Eagles are one of my favorite singing groups, and I keep one of their CDs in my truck for when I want really good driving music.

We stopped to stand on the corner in Winslow Arizona, as I bet millions have. After the photo op on the corner and in front of Don Henley's statue, it was on for a night's rest.

STANDING ON THE CORNER...

All my fellow travelers were up as early as I was the next morning, as this was to be *the day*. They were going to get to see Grand Canyon. But they were also excited that they were going to visit something with me for my first time, which is a rarity. On the route to the Canyon there are two places I had seen on maps but never stopped in my haste to get to Grand Canyon. I really suspect many people have done the same thing and bypassed them.

The first is Sunset Crater Volcano. This is a very recent volcano in geologic time and is part of that growing southern section of the Rocky Mountains. The lava flows we saw north of I-40 the day before were also a part of this same system. The Rockies are actually made up of three different types of rock: sedimentary in Canada, granite in the mid-section, and volcanic based in the southern parts. Geologic changes happen slowly in our lifeline, but can actually make changes fairly quickly in historic times. This system could easily become active again in my lifetime, or it could wait hundreds of years.

During our visit we climbed to the top of a cinder cone vent and recent activity (in geologic time) was evident everywhere. While this place can be easily overlooked, it is worth the stop.

Next was a visit to the Wupatki National Monument just north of the crater. This ancient Native American ruin is somewhat similar but has vast differences from the cliff dwellings I visited at Mesa Verde, as well as others. Each time I visit such places, I try to picture in my mind how the people lived. Each time I conclude that, while there are big cultural differences, we have a lot in common They struggled to feed and clothe their families, loved their women and children, grieved at the loss of a loved one, laughed at something funny, and generally did the best they could in their circumstances. In spite of all the outward differences, all mankind share these traits as human beings.

In the late morning we entered Grand Canyon National Park. While Diane had visited the north rim and Lowell had seen it as a youngster, it was a first for Mindy and the kids. As always, when I have visited the Canyon with someone for their first time, they have that reaction and look of wonder. It's almost like they just can't see enough and what they are seeing is almost unbelievable. There are many pictures, paintings, and movies of the Grand Canyon, but nothing prepares you for that awesome grandeur. Times like this are a reward all their own for me.

For the rest of the afternoon we gawked, walked, and explored the south rim. Our rooms were in Maswick Lodge, which is just a motel set in the park and nothing special. However, we didn't plan on doing anything but sleep and shower there anyway. Several of the older lodges along the rim have lots of character, but my choice for a longer stay at the Grand Canyon would be the lodge on the North Rim.

That evening my son-in-law Lowell got even on the Tucson meal. Supper was to be in the El Tovar dining room. Quite often you have a high-priced place, it is just that, high priced, but El Tovar does live up to its reputation with great food, service, and view. After I paid the bill, Lowell and I were basically even.

After our meal, we headed out for one of my favorite things while traveling—to watch a sunset. I still think that no matter how good ocean sunsets are, there is nothing like a sunset in the canyon lands. Maybe it is the pollution from the west coast or the reflections from the canyon itself, but Grand Canyon sunsets are often spectacular. I still think the Bryce Canyon sunsets are more impressive, maybe just because it is a smaller venue with more vivid colors in the canyon. Early the next morning, Diane and I hit the rim to see the sunrise. I have never thought the sunrises at the Canyon are as impressive as sunsets—

maybe it is because they seem to evolve more slowly and the light just filters down into the canyon.

With the rest of the morning spent exploring the South Rim, we headed south. Unless we actually descended into the canyon, we had seen quite a bit in just one full day. Our flight was scheduled for the next afternoon, but there was one more place to see. Although we didn't get to see much, we did a little exploring around Sedona before heading on to our rooms for the night. For my taste, what I saw was a little too touristy, but Mindy and Lowell want to return and spend time there. The red rock country and canyons are really different and unique. If you had the right place to stay or camp away from the more developed area, it may be a good place to spend some time

That night we stayed in Scottsdale at the Best Western. While it was part of a chain, it is locally owned and operated. Under the new owner/manager there had been a complete renovation, and she was particularly devoted to the inner courtyard. The courtyard at the Smugglers in Tucson was nice, but this was even more attractive and developed. The cost was more than reasonable for the area for what it offered.

With a morning of leisure and a good lunch, we boarded our flight home. Each of us returned with life-long memories in common and knew, though short, it was a great trip and time together. You never know what life may bring, so do it while you can.

JACKSON-CANTRILL EXPEDITION

The trips with Mindy and family were becoming a regular event. We had a great time, and they are great to travel with. Diane and I just did our extended weekends a couple of times a year, and I was still doing the cattle association tours. When talking during the winter, two places both Mindy and Taylor kept mentioning they would like to visit were Mount Rushmore and Yellowstone. I began looking at the practicality (mostly finances) of developing a trip that way.

What came out of the searching and planning became the Jackson-Cantrill expedition. The biggest problem was how to work in both places without driving too much and still see as much as possible. For me, a perfectly planned road trip allows you to cover some mileage and plan things to see or do so that you never drive more than a two-hour stretch without an interesting stop. It is also important to build in enough slack for serendipitous discoveries along the way and still get to your night stop with time to relax for a swim or just chill out. And in twenty-five years of cattle association tours, along with a lifetime of personal travel, it's not bragging to say I've become pretty good at it. I try to confine any really long days to the first day when excitement is high or the last day when you are looking forward to getting home.

Looking over the maps, it appeared to me that if we could fly in to either Denver or Salt Lake City and make a loop up and around, returning from the one we didn't fly in to, it would fill the bill. Of course, in doing this you almost have to use Southwest Airlines, because they don't price differently for one-way or roundtrip. The other option is to get lucky and find one-way fares that aren't more than the roundtrip cost. I did have enough rapid rewards for three roundtrips or six one-ways using Southwest Airlines. If I could find a good price one-way, then we would have only minimal fees for the other leg.

Like for the trip to Arizona, persistence pays. For nearly two months I would look on the Internet for one-way deals to either city. People think it takes lots of time, but not really. When checking e-mail or looking for some info on the web, it only takes a couple of minutes extra to do some quick price checks. It's kind of like being a salesman in that the more contacts you make, the higher the likelihood you succeed. No matter how many times you strikeout, just keep trying. Except for things that you will absolutely have to pay for even if you cancel, I keep looking for a better deal, but just not as hard when I am fairly satisfied with what I have confirmed. A good example is when I went on a visit to see my son's family in Tampa a couple of years ago. Before we left I had gone through two sets of air reservations and three rental cars and ended up saving about one hundred and fifty dollars. Unless you are with an airline that will issue a full value voucher, it's not possible, but certainly it is with cars or rooms. While a savings of five dollars to ten dollars one time isn't much compared to total travel cost, do that a few times and it adds up.

It took over two months of shopping for airfares until it hit. Luckily, we had a two to three day window for departure and return. It turned out that we found a really early Saturday morning flight where we could get to Denver for seventy-nine dollars, including fees one-way. That deal didn't show up on Travelocity or any of the other general search places, just on the American Airlines website. Another plus was that it was the same fare from either Louisville or Lexington. As I knew we would be coming back to Louisville on Southwest, Diane and I were to leave from there, while Mindy's family would leave from Lexington where they live. A friend would pick them up at our place when we returned.

The naming of this trip as the Jackson-Cantrill expedition is a poor knock-off of the Lewis and Clark expedition. But it was appropriate, as we would be leaving near the same place they started and visiting several of the same places they had. On Saturday morning we left from different airports, meeting up in Chicago for the same flight to Denver. Our flight arrived about nine-thirty in the morning, Mountain Daylight Time, so we had lots of time to start the road trip that day. Heading east on I-76, we almost made it back to where I met the drunken lady with the big cat several years before (and I had to tell the story again). At Fort Morgan we turned north on Route 52 to join Route 71 near the Pawnee National Grasslands. This was the first experience for Mindy's family in the western high plains. Personally, I find lots to look at, but you have to be observant and look for the subtle, or else it is just a long hot drive.

Lunch was in Scottsbluff. It was just about impossible to talk Diane out of stopping at Cabela's (the original store), which is a favorite of hers. But I knew once she started we would be lucky to get out of Nebraska by dark. Despite protest, I managed to just point it out as a drive-by that day. A little north we passed through Crawford, where many years before I had one of the wildest Fourth of July's in my life—rodeo, kids shooting bottle rockets at each other on horseback, and a dance lasting most of the night, only to get fired up again the next morning. At that time it was a town with about a thousand population invaded by five thousand people from miles around ready to party and celebrate. Old memories can be good!

On north through Hot Springs, South Dakota, and in to Wind Cave National Park, which is set in the southern end of the Black Hills. It's a beautiful drive with Buffalo herds, Antelope, and other wildlife that were all a first for my fellow travelers, outside of a zoo. Like that trip with the cattle association years before, there just weren't enough photo op stops to suit them, despite my assurance that there would be plenty of opportunities to see many more. At least this time I recognized that the enthusiasm was why we were doing this anyway. After a short photo op at the Crazy Horse Sculpture and Mt. Rushmore (there was going to be a visit for the lighting that night and an in-depth visit in the morning), it was on to our motel. It was time to stop, as it had been a long day already.

Our motel had a good view of the sculpture, and Diane and I were able to lie on our bed and watch the sun change the faces. It was a decent place to stay, and Mindy and Diane both liked that there was Starbucks coffee along with a souvenir mug in the room. For me, I don't particularly like Starbucks, but did like a good room with a view at a reasonable price. I was bushed after a long day, so I passed on the night visit and was content to watch the sunset from comfort. Actually, we did get to see the lighting from a distance, and it is pretty spectacular. Diane and I saw the lighting up a few years before.

The next morning was the best visit I have experienced at Mt Rushmore. We made an early start before the tour buses arrived and had an almost blustery morning that also cut the number of people there. This made for a visit with fewer people than any time I've been there since the Two Boys West trip.

I mentioned earlier that the grandkids got to make a visit with one of the original workers on the sculpture. Had there been a crowd, I doubt if they would have been able to just sit and talk with him. After we had been there about an hour, an early morning thunderstorm broke across the top of the presidents' heads, complete with small hail and cold winds. It was not a big storm and was short-lived, but impressive nevertheless. One of our goals was accomplished.

As I usually do, the route on west was not the interstate but old US 16 west to New Castle, Wyoming, and then up to I-90 at Moorcroft. At Buffalo we stopped to pick up picnic stuff for lunch later. Then at Sheridan we departed the interstate again on Route 331 to pick up US 14 A at Dayton—relief, back on the less crowded way. That afternoon was to be one of my favorite drives across the Bighorn Mountains.

Much of the drive you see only a few travelers and many great vistas and can stop for a snowball fight in July. However, this time Diane had a memorable highlight. She, after many years, finally got to see a real live moose grazing beside the road. Also along that route is the Medicine Wheel that many believe is the Native American version of Stonehenge. Cattle run on open range there, and it is not unusual to have to run them out of your way to proceed. The cattle are moved from the valleys to the mountains by either truck or old-fashioned trail drive to spend the summer on mountain meadows. This was a first for the younger folks.

After passing Bighorn Lake, we followed the Shoshone River down through Powell to Cody. I always try to educate my fellow travelers on the crops they see as we go along and often stop for a closer look. This route provided the first opportunity to show them sugar beets that are still a major sugar source, and, for the grower, the vegetative tops make excellent cattle feed. After a day of seeing new things, we rolled in to Cody.

My choice of a place to stay was again the Buffalo Bill Cabins. I think Mindy questioned my judgment when we first arrived when she saw the exterior. But after she got to see inside, the rustic looking cabins quickly changed her mind. That night we were going to a rodeo.

The regular Cody night rodeo is not a particularly top-end event, but is a great experience for some green horns. Fortunately, Diane and I didn't have the same experience of about freezing that evening. The rodeo that night had a lot better cowboys and critters than the last time we stopped. The young cowboys particularly impressed Ashley. At least she took a bunch of pictures and concentrated on the goings on. I had wondered what the *city slickers'* reaction would be to a rodeo, but no fear, they had a ball.

Daylight the next morning found me at Wal-Mart to stock up on our picnic supplies. We were heading to our second major goal of the trip that day, Yellowstone.

I again chose the route through Dead Indian Pass and down into one of the world's largest super volcano's caldera. We spent the day visiting Tower Falls, Yellowstone Falls, and stopping to take lots of pictures of the wildlife. We even got to see a bear and her cubs along the way and had a great picnic lunch alongside a small mountain stream. A little about this bunches' picture taking—while I occasionally take pictures, they seem to be full-time photographers. Diane, Mindy, and Ashley all have good digital cameras, and Diane takes her laptop along to download, cull, and put the keepers on a disk, making it possible to take even more pictures. They had taken a lot on the two previous trips but informed me that this time they had over three hundred by the time we reached Yellowstone. As I have talked about before, Yellowstone doesn't immediately overwhelm you the way the Grand Canyon, Yosemite, or Crater Lake might, but grows almost beyond imagination.

For that evening my planning had not been too good. Starting so late making reservations, we couldn't get rooms in Yellowstone that night but did find a good place down in Teton Village. It was not a big problem as it is beautiful drive down beside the Teton Mountains. I did want them to visit Jackson Hole and see the elk herds, ski slopes, and maybe even ride a slide down the mountain. However, before we got to our hotel, they thought I had lost it and was lost. The road I took went from a good two lane, to a rough two lane, to narrow gravel, and the questions began.

"Are you sure this is the way?"

I had found a gray road, which is almost always preferable to the more beaten path. We did make it, and we were never lost in spite of their doubts.

Jackson Hole, Wyoming, has a beautiful setting, some neat shops, and way too much tourist stuff for my taste. In my mind, it is overpriced and overcrowded. We thought we would have a good supper there, but found the menus too pricey and the places too crowded. Mindy came through—on our way down from Teton Village, she had spotted Calico, an Italian restaurant, and suggested we go back and try that. That night we had an excellent meal at a decent price and some of the best Bruschetti I ever had at a restaurant.

The next morning loading up to head back to Yellowstone, we had a treat as a flock of hot air balloons cruised along the mountains and landed in the valley near our hotel. Today was to be geyser day. We planned to spend all day walking amongst the geyser, stretching out below the Old Faithful area. Not getting a particularly early start, the Old Faithful area was already starting to get crowded, but we persisted. And it was not just people that we dodged during our wanderings, but buffalo and elk as well. By late afternoon I was about walked out, and even the youngsters were ready for a break.

Back across the continental divide, we went to Grant Village, where we had rooms for the night. The rooms were a little culture shock for the kids and their parents since there was no TV and no AC, but they adapted and did have cell phone service. Little did they know what I had planned a couple of nights later.

That evening we decided to dine very casually at the snack bar/pizza place down by the lake. This proved to be a very entertaining evening at Gmama's expense. After a couple of glasses of wine at the high altitude, she became a little flighty (a small buzz). Ashley can almost always get her to laughing, and it worked better than usual. To make it worse, I actually needed to go outside to feed my nicotine addiction, but told them I just had to get away, as everybody was looking.

In passing a table not too far away I commented (fairly loudly), "I wonder what's wrong with those people?" referring to the bunch I just left. That only increased the hilarity as they thought I was escaping.

So now when Ashley does her crack up Gmama routine, it comes out—"Okay, Diane, that's enough wine," and we all crack up when she protest that it was all Ashley's fault. Nothing like an ongoing prank.

I was determined that my family would see Old Faithful during the quiet without standing ten people deep. Before daylight the next morning, I became the cruel tour guide, rolling everybody up and heading back across the continental divide again. We made it in time to see Old Faithful erupting in predawn light with less than one hundred people joining us. Finally, a place opened up for coffee and some breakfast. I am one of those few people who like to roll out of bed directly to coffee and something to eat, but it was worth the delay.

For this day we planned to finish visiting a couple of the basins we missed the day before and wander up to Norris Basin and eventually Mammoth Hot Springs. We surely missed something we should have seen but did a pretty good job of seeing a little more than just the high-lights of Yellowstone. Yellowstone could win the vote as the place we would most like to revisit. I especially want to make it in winter someday (so much to see and so little time).

A little less than a two-hour drive put us at our stop for the night in Three Forks, Montana. Our place to stay was to be the Broken Spur motel. It was not a fancy place but clean, comfortable, and well maintained. It is owned and operated by the Stratton family. He is a semi-retired geologist, and she manages the motel. When I asked about places to eat, they mentioned a place a few miles east at Logan called The Land of Magic. Off the main road, up a gravel street, and there it is. Rustic and warm looking from the outside, it doesn't appear too special; however, the one thing special there is the food. We all had perhaps the best steak supper there I have experienced, no matter the setting or price. And I have tried a lot. Ranchers, who wanted to have a good steakhouse locally, started it, like the Little Apple Brewery in Manhattan, Kansas. It is not glamorous or glitzy, just great food and service in a comfortable atmosphere. Recently, I have seen it rated in the top five steakhouses in America. It's amazing what you find down a gravel road sometimes.

The next morning at the complimentary breakfast, it was just as rewarding at the Broken Spur. The food was just okay, but the conversation was great! All of us, especially Diane, have an interest in geology and the earth. Mr. Stratton proved to be a fountain of knowledge about the area. A lifetime of working as a geologist and recently conducting geological tours provided a background to pass on a lot. Breakfast time that morning extended well over an hour. Diane left with a gift, some unusual rocks for her classroom (luggage was getting heavier all the time).

The plans for that day ended up being a bust. A couple of times Diane and I visited the Sunlight Goldmine near Whitehall and I had been able to get in by contacting the local county agent. Unfortunately for us, it had recently changed owners and was undergoing personnel changes, so no visitors were allowed at that time. It is an impressive sight; I wish the kids could have visited. Maybe next time.

With that cancellation, I called ahead to see if we could check in to our next night's place early. Yep, we could. A couple of years before, Diane and I, on a cattlemen tour, visited the Sitz Ranch in the Big Hole country west of Dillon Montana. I had hopes of my younger ones meeting a real ranch family about their age. The Sitz are an outstanding family, who has a worldwide reputation for the ranch started by their parents. It's nothing fancy, just great people and great cattle in an unbelievably beautiful setting. But it was the middle of haying season where work days in the field run daylight to dark, so it wasn't convenient for an extended visit.

Looking for a place to stay near Dillon, I came across the Jackson Hot Springs Lodge in Jackson, Montana. We saw the small town in the distance before turning off when we visited the Sitz Ranch before and had no idea that a place to stay would be there. The pictures and price on the Internet looked good, so I booked us two cabins for the night. Had my son-in-law Lowell realized that not only was there not a TV, AC, or even cell phone service, he may have balked due to techno withdrawal. But he is pretty tolerant and did have his DVD player loaded with old TV shows, so he could survive. Proving that opposites attract, Mindy loved it.

For me, the Jackson Hot Springs Lodge is a place where I could go to spend some time relaxing. Cabins prices are very reasonable; there is a bar, a big dance floor for the cowboys who come to town on Saturday nights, and a gourmet chef. To top it all off, they have their own naturally heated pool, supplied by the local hot spring, that actually heats the whole town, along with the lodge and cabins. Nearby there is great trout fishing in the Big Hole River; ski slopes are also nearby, as well as miles of gravel roads to explore. What else could I want? I don't need to be entertained to have a great relaxing time. The Lewis and Clark expedition two centuries before had also used Jackson and the hot springs as a resting place.

That afternoon Mindy, Ashley, and I explored some of those gravel roads, made a short visit out to Sitz Ranch, then watched a crew constructing a massive log gate entrance to a new million dollar house that was being built in the middle of nowhere for an invader from the west coast to use as a summer home.

For the Big Hole country, the weather was hot. Diane kept saying that with no AC we would burn up that night. So being the good husband, I got all the windows open and a cross breeze flowing. About eleven at night she woke me up to close the windows and find the extra blankets. So much for needing AC; it's natural. I'd bet there isn't more than one night every two years when air conditioning would feel good.

The hot springs pool is great. Local ranchers, who often come in to relax in the warm water, joined us. After a soak in the pool, we had a great supper of local trout fixed to perfection. Just like the Lewis and Clark expedition two hundred years before, the Big Hole proved to be a good stop. Even with a night's sleep broken up by a shivering wife, we had a great, if too short of a stay at Jackson Hot Springs Lodge. It is someplace we would like to go, stay a few days, and really explore those gravel roads.

The next day we crossed Chief Joseph Pass into Idaho. That day we planned to visit Craters of the Moon National Monument. So we headed down US 9 along the Salmon River and through Arco. Craters of the Moon, like Sunset Crater in Arizona that we had visited that spring, is a recent lava flow in geologic time. It is part of the total Yellowstone volcanic system and would have been active while the Native Americans were already on the continent.

It is easier to see and get around than Sunset Crater was and even afforded an opportunity to look down in to a vent. Even though created by heat, there was still snow packed down in the vent hole. I had visited here a couple of times, and this was a place Diane definitely wanted to see again. There is no rock collecting allowed in the park so she had to wait until we were out of the park to collect some samples for her classroom.

Our reservations for that night were in Twin Falls, but in spite of a good, long visit at the Craters, we were going to arrive early. The decision was made to head on south into Nevada. What was left on our trip plans was to see the Great Salt Lake and go spend a day at Park City. Mindy had a longtime friend there who Diane almost considered another daughter.

Lowell was driving, so right on through Jackpot we went and down to Wells. While there is not a lot in Wells, I convinced him to stop, as there was practically nothing east until we got to Salt Lake City. We checked into a so-so motel and headed for supper at the Flying J Truck Stop and Casino. The food was typical, but the gaming tables were generous, as Lowell won enough in a few minutes to buy our supper and have some left over.

Heading east the next morning, we didn't move nearly as fast as I had about forty-five years earlier heading west while my brother slept. But we did move on. Bonneville Salt Flats and the Great Salt Lake are another of those places that are hard to describe, and pictures just don't do justice to them. This wouldn't be someplace to spend much time unless you had a particular purpose. The stark contrast from about anyplace else I've ever visited makes it unique.

From Salt Lake we headed in to the Wasatch Range and arrived at Park City shortly after noon. Mindy hooked up with her friend Heather, while the rest of us explored a little. Park City, while a very typical ski/tourist town, has kept much of the flavor of my visit decades ago. Maybe I just saw it that way, but it did not seem as plastic and fake as many of the places. In our exploration we decided there were a couple of things we just had to do: ride the zip line and slide at the Olympic Park. The balance of the afternoon involved a dip in the pool, followed with a good meal in town and a visit at Heather's place, located on a hill above the city. It is always nice to visit old friends.

In the morning Diane and I were up early to do some more poking around until the rest of the bunch got up to make a short visit to see downtown Salt Lake. Our plans were to do the zip line and slide that afternoon.

Now we have some zip lines around here but none that run thousands of feet down the mountain. At the Olympic Park, there is the short version and the long version. While this old man and the kids were off for an adventure, Diane found a place to watch pre-Olympians practice ski jumping into a pool. She would in no way ever ride a ski lift, let alone allow herself to dangle by a harness way up in the air. Our first ride was the low version that involved riding the ski lift up about two thousand feet, getting harnessed up, and then bracing yourself against a starting gate. Popping out, you drop into almost nothingness and roll down the hill, dangling from a cable. It's probably not as fast or as long as it seems. The buffer-breaking system brings you to a fairly gentle stop.

Before I got on, a man just slightly younger than me said, "It was more fun than I've had since being a kid."

It is a little adrenaline rush, but not too wild.

What I really wanted to do was ride the slide. The slide is like a bobsled or luge run on wheels in a winding metal trough down the mountain. For this one, it is a ski lift ride to about four thousand feet above the valley, then aboard the one-man sled for a fast, almost two-mile ride, winding down the mountain. This was a blast! The only problem was that both my son-in-law Lowell and grandson Taylor had beat me down, even though we started at the same time. Nothing would do but a rematch.

Up the mountain we headed and on to the slides. A quick breakaway with Gpapa in the lead, I was determined not to use the brake all the way down this time. About halfway down, with the different tracks wandering around corners and trees, I did it. Leaning too much into a curve, the slide flipped out from under me, while I continued to slide down the metal track. The only thing I could think of at that moment was *wipeout,* and that old surfer song ran through my head. Friction makes a pretty good brake, so I finally stopped sliding, no worse for wear other than a few floor burns on my arm and elbows. Then walking back up, I put the slide back in the track and slowly cruised on down, still wanting to sing "Wipeout."

At the bottom, both son-in-law and grandson greeted me with, "Where've you been?"

They at least hadn't observed my *wipeout.* At first, I just wanted to tell them somebody slowed me down.

Finally and reluctantly, I had to tell the truth, especially when they asked what happened to my elbow.

Okay, that was enough adventure for one day for the old pensioner, but the youngsters had one more thing to do—ride the big zip line. This one goes up the four thousand feet to where the slide starts. Just as they reached the top, a summer mountain thunderstorm started up the back of the mountain, which required a quick run to shelter. There they were on a mountaintop and couldn't ride the zip line, slide down, or ski lift down with the lightening nearby. After about an hour, the weather was not showing much hope of clearing soon, so a ranger in an SUV headed up a back road to bring the stranded ones down. We had quite an afternoon of adventure for both young and old—a great way to about finish up a great trip.

The only thing left was to go buy more luggage for souvenirs (including rocks) and head out early the next morning to catch our flight home. We had acquired several pounds of rocks, over one thousand pictures (before editing), and a huge load of beautiful memories.

CRUISING AND CRAB CAKES

We have now come to the point in 2007 when I planned our Grey Roads and Gluttony tour in the Midwest. That title and the memories it stirred prompted me to begin this story of journeys through a lifetime. However, just about three days before we planned to leave on an eight-day jaunt through southern Missouri, the Flint Hills of Kansas, and the cornfields of Iowa, I received a phone call.

My friend John in Rhode Island wondered if we might come up and cruise Newport Harbor. The tall ships would be there, and he had checked with his cousin so that we could do a day cruise around Narragansett Bay, similar to what we had done before on a *side trip*. I let him know that plans were already made for our daughter's family and ourselves, but if I could get everything canceled out, we would give it a shot.

There's nothing like informing the *girls* that instead of cowboy boots and jeans, the appropriate attire would be deck shoes and shorts. However, they are flexible and made a quick adjustment, even if I didn't give them time to shop.

Out of this trip came what has become a running joke with Mindy. The evening before we were to go on our harbor cruise and visit the tall ships, she made the mistake we have teased her about ever since.

She asked, "John, what is appropriate to wear cruising?"

Now I had experienced his very subtle, dry, absolutely funny sense of delivering off-the-wall humor.

His reply was, "Cute boat clothes." This was very seriously stated without him cracking a smile.

However, the rest of us cracked up, as Mindy pondered (having no previous frame of reference) just what cute boat clothes were. So it has become a tradition whenever we talk about where she is going, like last winter to Park City Utah, I had to ask, "You have cute ski clothes?" even though she wasn't skiing. Or when on a trip taking in a ghost tour I asked, "You have cute ghost clothes?" And it's not the joke, but the memories that question brings to mind that is important.

Early in the morning (seems we always start really early) we rolled out on what I know is not really my favorite type of traveling. Our route for the most part was interstates, complete with semis and rush hours. But unless you have more time than we did, time was important. After a night spent north of Harrisburg, Pennsylvania, we pulled into John and Ellen's in the early afternoon. The only interesting parts of the drive were the ride along the Houstanic River in Connecticut and following old US 1 on into Rhode Island. We did have a photo op at Mystic Pizza.

Diane and I were staying at our host home and luckily (if not cheaply) found a nearby motel for the kids. That evening we had a great time grilling the steaks I had brought along, and had lots of serious tale swapping. John and Ellen had spent time with Ashley and met Mindy and Lowell, but just in passing. Sometimes it's not easy for younger folks to really enjoy visiting and getting to know older ones, but they really got along great. And John and I didn't tell too many lies or too many boring stories.

The next day we took everybody down to visit Mystic Seaport, then had an afternoon of just chilling out. Our cruise of Narragansett Bay was to be the next day. Unless you just don't like boats and water, it's hard not to enjoy a day of sightseeing around the Bay and Newport Harbor. Along the way, you get a different view of how the upper crust lives.

We began in Jamestown, cruised Newport Harbor, and made a circle around the end of the island and back. John's cousin's home is just beside the home that John grew up in and less than a block from the marina. We got the opportunity to walk through Jamestown and do a little exploring. Just like Diane and I experienced previously, it was not just the seeing and doing that made it worthwhile, but the truly warm hospitality and friendship.

After another great evening, we scheduled an early start on Saturday morning. I had been talked in to spending most of the day in New York City. I had been there when much younger, gotten stranded by fog on a canceled flight, and taken a bus, subway, and a taxis around in the city, but really had decided that without a specific purpose, such as for a play, museum, or something, it was not my kind of town. It just doesn't feel like a place I can go in to and wander and explore. One of my most vivid early memories was of being banged by an old lady's umbrella as I was trying to step aside to let her on the bus first. But when the daughter and granddaughter ask, they usually get their way.

We made Times Square about nine-thirty in the morning and proceeded to explore, while being assailed by street vendors. Maybe sometime I will go and be guided by somebody that really knows the city and enjoy it. Actually, there were two things that I really wanted to do. One was visit the site of the 9/11 tragedy, and the other was to take the boat out to the Statue of Liberty.

That afternoon we accomplished both. Getting back from Liberty Island about five-thirty in the evening, we headed west on I-78.

While we weren't particularly looking for a great restaurant, we did find one in Easton, Pennsylvania. It was listed in a AAA guide, so we stopped, as it had been a long day with a crappy lunch, and we were ready to sit down for a t decent meal. The Riverside Café in Easton proved to be one of the better places I have eaten. It had a good menu selection and excellent service. What a fitting way to about wrap up another great day on the road.

Driving on to after dark, we stayed at the same motel just north of Harrisburg that we had stayed in coming up. Thankfully, Lowell thrives on driving and driving in traffic. I could have made it, but wouldn't be worth shooting after that. Sunday we headed back to the real world. There were no rocks but many pictures and more memories of Taylor with a cool new skateboard and Ashley with a fake purse purchased in New York City.

A big personal reward on our trips is getting to spend time with three generations of the family. We get to enjoy each other much more than just at a quick family gathering on a holiday. It provides another step to building memories that will live on long after I am gone.

DOWN THE RIVER

Well it wasn't exactly down the river, but pretty close. For several generations Kentucky products (especially whiskey) moved down the Ohio and Mississippi River to be sold in New Orleans.

This year Mindy would get to be an only child for a trip. Lowell was tied up with business, Ashley was furthering her budding singing career, and Taylor was working for gas and spending money. In addition, we had a long weekend wedding to attend up in West Virginia in late summer, and I got talked in to doing another cattle association tour the last week of June. So it was that with Diane doing summer school and Mindy scheduling several weeks of summer dance camps, the only free time was the first full week of June. Time limited what we could do and where we could go.

We narrowed our choices down to two places that we had enjoyed, and Mindy had never been to San Antonio or New Orleans. San Antonio would require flying, and right then airfares were almost prohibitive, so the Crescent City won by default. It was the fall before Katrina and Rita that I had last visited the area, so I was curious as to what was going on.

This is how Mindy became an only child traveling with us. Our route wouldn't be down the rivers, but rather the way that the early whiskey traders came home. We would take the Natchez Trace to at least to around Jackson, Mississippi. By the way, I did remember to ask Mindy if she had cute New Orleans clothes to wear (and she did).

A request that Diane had was to find a place to stay in the French Quarter. We had visited before, but had never stayed right in the thick of things, preferring to commute from the more outlying areas or across on the west bank in Belle Chasse. A few years ago, I sent my oldest son, Sean, on his honeymoon to New Orleans and had found the Hotel St. Marie on Toulouse Street just north of Bourbon. He reported that it was really nice, and the staff was very helpful, especially for the cost in what can be a high-price city.

On Monday morning we headed south to Nashville to pick up the Natchez Trace Parkway. I have driven it all, but never on one trip and didn't this time. With a speed limit of forty-five, it is a little slower than many would like; however, with fuel prices and the fact it is a little shorter, the extra time seemed worth it. The Natchez Trace is a beautiful drive during the spring redbud and dogwood bloom and again in the fall colors. In early June, it is a green tunnel but still a relaxing drive. We managed to have a picnic lunch and stop along the way at highlights and historical points, like Meriwether Lewis's grave, Indian Mounds, and more. With no towns, stoplights, or traffic tie-ups, more miles are covered quicker than you might think.

After a night at Kosciusko, Mississippi, we again got an early start south. This time we got off the Trace and took Mississippi Route 35 down in to Louisiana. I drove this road years before when accompanying my friend Roy down to take a load of stuff to his parents near Columbia. The route was as I remembered a mix of rolling hills, forest, and farmland. Again, it wasn't a pedal-to-the-metal road, but you can roll right along, and it's certainly more interesting than following eighteen-wheelers down an interstate. Just north of Lake Ponchartrain, I topped the tank with diesel and had averaged over 22 mpg on the way down. That's pretty good for a big crew cab F-250. On the way back following only interstates for speed, we only made 18 mpg.

The causeway across Ponchartrain runs about twenty-four miles across to New Orleans. I wanted to go in this way to get a good view of the skyline going in. We made it downtown before noon and gave Mindy a neat intro to what, for me, makes the city special. Sitting in the French Market Café eating crawfish pie, watching the people, and listening to a really good blues/jazz band is what it's all about. One of the things I immediately noticed was that nothing was as crowded as on my visits before.

After lunch we cruised some shops, people watched, visited the cathedral and museum, and finally headed for our hotel. As Sean had reported, the St. Marie is in a super location and has a great staff. It's not overly fancy but quite good enough, with balconies overlooking a courtyard and pool. Diane rested, Mindy read, and I did a little more exploring. We had plans for that first night on the town.

One of the places that the ladies wanted to go was for a brunch at the Court of Two Sisters, so we did a light evening meal there, and they got reservations for the next morning. Another one of the things Mindy most wanted to do was go on a ghost tour. She had done one in Charleston, South Carolina, before and wanted to do one in New Orleans. So at eight o'clock in the evening, just as it was growing dark, we started. New Orleans is reported to be one of the most haunted cities, with heinous murders, voodoo, and various atrocities. I still don't know if it is haunted, but the tour was certainly entertaining, with lots of great stories and some insight to the city history.

It was a great start to the evening. With the tour ending just across the street from Pat O'Brien's, nothing would do but to have a hurricane. New Orleans is one of the few places I have been; you can just wander around, drink in hand, and pop in and out of nightclubs. Now I had an agenda as well. I really like both blues and jazz, and one of the people I wanted to see was Big Al Carson, who performs at the Funky Pirate on Bourbon Street. So after taking in a little of Preservation Hall and looking in at a couple more places, I finally get us to the Funky Pirate.

The featured drink there is the hand grenade. Well the ladies just had to try one, as their hurricanes were about gone. I settled for a Diet Coke, because I figured somebody should be able to find the hotel. Big Al didn't disappoint, and we stayed for a full set. Mindy is a dancer, and when music is good she wants to move along with it (can't sit still), especially after a hurricane and half of a hand grenade. She was dressed in cute New Orleans clothes that night, and just before the set ended Big Al looked over and said, "Hey, pretty lady, come on up here."

Even cold stone sober she isn't shy and will welcome a chance to perform. However, it wasn't an on-stage performance, but Big Al needed a tip jar girl. Mindy proceeded to work the crowd, and I think folks thought it was a setup, as she almost danced around to pass the jar. It's just a shame she wasn't on commission, as the jar was full when she finished.

MINDY AND BIG AL CARSON

We made a stop at another place with a really good, full band playing classic and modern rock, and a final stop with an 80s music band that I found too loud but still great, and I finally got the girls home safe. As always, I was up early and walking just past daybreak, and several places were still swinging, guys were wandering out of strip bars, and cleanup was beginning for another day. One of the things I noticed was that the nightclub area, especially along Bourbon Street, seems to be cleaner and not near as smelly as the times I visited before.

The second day started with the ladies doing brunch at the Court of Two Sisters, while I went exploring. Often I have found riding city buses, trams, and trolleys is a cheap, interesting way to explore. So while they brunched, I rode and looked. At this point if all I did was ride into town to the French Quarter or Business or Arts Districts,

I would have said things were moving back toward normal after the hurricanes. The next day, as we were heading out, it occurred to me that with the total extent of the damage it would be a very long time, if ever, before it came close to being the same again.

The afternoon saw us do another thing we wanted to do—visit one of the old cemeteries. We ended up going to St Louis 1, which is west of the French Quarter. Riding the trolley, we only had a few blocks to walk, which was enough in the ninety plus heat and humidity. If you have never been to New Orleans and visited a cemetery, it is a revelation with all the graves above ground. The amazing thing is that there seem to be a lot of people in these above ground crypts in so small of an area. For this particular cemetery, the other thing that surprised me was the large number of German ancestry names represented there. I guess in an older one like this I expected more French names, but this one had very few. Many of the inscriptions showed that the older ones were actually born in Germany in the early 1800s.

After the night before, I was ready to party again, but couldn't convince my fellow travelers to make it another night. Catching a cab, we headed to Mulatte's Cajun, which not only featured Cajun food, but music and dance. It wasn't long on ambience, but both the food and music were pretty good, even though I have had both better out in the southwestern part of the state in small town bars and restaurants.

Thursday was a day that I had been looking forward to since thinking about this trip. The fall before the hurricanes Katrina and Rita, I put together a tour to east Texas and Louisiana for our cattle association. We made stops in the southwestern part of Louisiana on ranches, with the Corps of Engineers and NRCS along the river, and spent a day in Plaquemine Parrish with the local extension agent Allen Vaughn.

Plaquemine adjoins New Orleans and starts on the west bank, which is actually south, and runs both sides of the Mississippi River all the way to its mouth. While actually wider in places, they like to say it is a mile wide and over eighty miles long. Surprisingly, there is (or was) a good mix of agriculture and fisheries in the Parrish, with several herds of beef cattle, a sizable citrus industry (Satsuma, navels, and pink grapefruit), and Cajun tomatoes were all commercially viable. In addition, there was a sizable industry for shrimp, oysters, and fish. While there is a definite Cajun influence, several in the fishing industry were descendants of Croatians from the Black Sea region, and in recent years several Vietnamese. In addition, many oil companies have facilities located there.

Allen has been the county agent there for over a quarter of a century, and his wife taught high school during this time. After the disaster caused by the hurricanes, we contacted him only to learn that he had evacuated safely, but his home in Port Sulfur was a total loss. The only thing salvageable was his wife's china. They escaped with a few pictures, clothes, and most importantly their lives. Our local cattlemen group, rather than contribute through an organization, sent some funds directly to Allen to be used where it was most needed. There is now a commercial grade washer dryer unit at their extension office. The local people used this in the cleanup effort.

We also sent funds to the family of my friend and fellow traveler Roy Toney, as his family is still in southern Mississippi, and while not as badly damaged as on the coast, they also suffered lots of damage. They purchased chainsaws to assist in cleanup. I guess I feel that, whenever possible, any contributions for a disaster are better targeted on a local level, with local people making the decisions.

So this Thursday with Diane and Mindy in tow, we joined Allen shortly before eight in the morning for a look at Plaquemine Parrish after the storms. One thing that had become apparent was that close to the river there was usually less damage because much of that area, including the older French Quarter, Business District, etc. and the West Bank are actually higher than much of the rest of the city. Most of the flooding in those areas was a result of the rain and pump failure, not the levee breaks.

As we headed down the river, at first there appeared to be a great recovery from the damage of the storms. I saw little changed from my earlier visit before the storms. Shortly after heading out of Belle Chasse, things began to change. It was almost like north of an imaginary line there was a little damage still evident, but south there was almost total non-recoverable destruction.

Allen was able to point out where the numerous levee breaks had occurred and what would likely never be restored. He had stories of boating down the still-flooded Parrish, seeing barges, boats, and houses that ended up far from where they had been, in the middle of the road or just gone. Later we visited with a beef producer who had lost his entire cowherd, and when he came back as soon as the storm passed, had to shoot several suffering cattle caught in the top of trees. Three years later, he was starting to rebuild.

Hurricane Katrina brought in many feet of river water, but Rita, not much later, brought in seawater that has killed most of the trees in the lower part of the Parrish, including most of the citrus.

Most of what we saw will never be rebuilt in Plaquemine Parrish. Commercial fishing boats still sat out in marshes and fields, either beyond repair or too costly to have them moved back to the water. There are lots of abandoned foundations, pieces of structures, and wild growth. Much of the fishing industry is cash in hand and just beyond subsistence, so many of the fishermen don't have any funds to start up again. Some of the older, more established, residents are returning, but almost two-thirds of the younger families have moved away permanently.

If they want to rebuild, the closest place for any supplies is at least a one-hour drive away, and there are almost no trades people except up close to New Orleans. Another problem for those wanting to rebuild is the cost of homeowners insurance. It now averages over nine thousand dollars per year. Most people returning are just putting in lower cost trailers and not insuring them.

Plaquemine Parrish and its local government did a much better job working with FEMA and other recovery efforts, so as a result its people were resettled in the temporary housing much quicker than in New Orleans.

Why? They did a better job of making codes, inspections, and setups much easier to *git 'er done*. Much of the recovery effort problems in some of the areas seemed to be the result of, not the outside effort, but the local establishment.

The bottom line is that things will never be the same again, and there will never be a true recovery in the foreseeable future. However, Allen and other locals like him are working, digging, exploring, and planning to make it a viable place for the future. It's different, but still a future when right now there is almost none.

In writing about this visit, I have found it hard to really tell about what I saw and felt. I just found myself at a loss for the words to express the experience. Even Diane was hesitant to take many pictures, saying she just felt strange doing so with all the damage and suffering.

One of the things that I did accomplish was to line up both wholesale shrimp and oysters to take home. I had put two freezers in the back of the truck for this purpose. These I plugged these in at the hotel parking on Thursday night so they would be cold before we picked up seafood Friday morning just before we headed North.

After a good fried oyster lunch at Salvia restaurant in Belle Chasse, it was back to the hotel. We had a good nap, then did some souvenir shopping and got ready for another highlight.

My taste in food has greatly expanded from the peanut butter and jelly sandwiches of my first visit to New Orleans. I heard my parents talk about eating at Antoine's in New Orleans and was aware of its reputation of being one of the great restaurants.

Mindy and I had scouted it out earlier in the week, while Diane was resting during the afternoon. While it was closed, the door was open and we walked in just to look and inquire. One of the managers greeted us, and we spent a few minutes visiting. He told us to be sure and come back and ask especially for Walter Chedda for our waiter. For our last night in New Orleans it seemed appropriate to finish up at one of the truly historic places, renowned for its great food and service.

The host seemed surprised when we requested a particular waiter and escorted us to our table. Walter was tied up with a large wedding reception, but almost immediately came over to visit and introduce us to Hugo, who would take care of us, plus he would periodically check on us. Service at Antoine's is as good as any I have ever experienced in my life. Later, in talking to a young trainee, I found out that it usually takes at least eighteen months of training before you became a *waiter*. At least four saw to our every need, with Walter Chedda checking to see if all was well.

Many of their dishes are world famous, and their chefs have been creating great recipes since the mid-1800s. Probably their most famous dish is Oysters Rockefeller, which is one that they have never released the recipe for. With a really good wine, Oysters Rockefeller, great entrees, and dessert, we partook of a superb meal. And the bill reflected this as well. Quite often I have felt that with many big reputation places where you end up with a large bill, they just don't deliver value, but Antoine's exceeded my expectations.

After the meal, our waiter treated us to a tour of the entire restaurant complex. It can host as many as eighteen hundred people, but always seemed a small, cozy place. Dozens of private and semi-private rooms are interspersed with small dining rooms. The restaurant occupies almost an entire city block. Their wine cellar alone is larger than many restaurants. Because of the hurricane, they had a wall failure and were closed for almost eighteen months, but their personnel had been kept on. This was a great way to finish up and remember our visit to New Orleans.

Before daylight the next morning, we headed back down in to Plaquemine Parrish to pick up our load of right-off-the-boat shrimp and oysters. Then it was a long drive north. We did see one more thing on our way out of the city. Quite a bit of the eastern side, including the ninth ward, is visible from the interstate, and like down in Plaquemine Parrish, it is a heart-rending sight. Even if I wanted to get a closer look, I probably wouldn't have. The area can be extremely unsafe, since during the few days we were there nine murders occurred in this area. This was a sad way to leave what had been one of my more enjoyable trips.

The rest of the trip home was just a drive with nothing to see except trees along the roadside and traffic. It wasn't until about Alabama that we saw anything of interest. Again, this brought home to me why I just don't like interstates. About the only advantage is they can be quicker, unless you hit a traffic jam. But they always seem to tire me out, and they seem longer.

Two months later as I looked back on this trip, I realized it was one of our most memorable ever. I continued to get to know our daughter better and was able to return to one of the cities I really like. Another thing that made this trip important was that at the time we really didn't know the status of Mindy's health. When I started writing about this trip, that status still had a big question mark, and I was hesitant to even mention it.

Just before the previous Christmas, she was diagnosed with thyroid cancer. And even though the doctors thought that the surgery and follow up radiation treatments had gone well, the next tests would not be done until early August. Needless to say, I probably wouldn't mention it now unless that had gone well, and it appears that the treatments were indeed successful, as nothing has shown up in any of the tests.

I hope that at some point before I get too old that we might spend some time on a road trip with each of our children where they are the only child. Most of the time, it is not just them, but us as well who are too busy and too involved with jobs, families, and communities to really have undivided time together and escape that everyday grind.

WINDING DOWN

Later the same year as our New Orleans trip, I set up what is likely the last cattle association tour I will do (never say never) and chose to make it to one of my favorite places to visit, Kansas.

The vast majority of people that have made a trek to or across Kansas will tell me that it is just a long, boring drive. However, in my opinion they never really looked. I made my first visits through Kansas on the trip I titled Two Boys West and several times on our way to Colorado. Each time I just couldn't see where most people came up with their opinion.

Since those times, I have ended up making visits quite often to buy cattle or revisit people who have become friends during my trips there. A conclusion that I have come to is that most often people that find it boring have never bothered to get off the interstate on to the less traveled roads.

I have come to really enjoy visiting in the Flint Hills and think that it is one of the most beautiful places in late spring with the rolling hills, blooming wild flowers, and belly-deep tall grass prairie, with small interesting towns and villages to explore.

And even better are the local people. They are a hardy bunch, close to the land, their families, and communities. My experience is that most are friendly, helpful, and almost always ready for a good conversation.

A stop I try to make is at Lyons Ranch outside of Manhattan. Jan, who is a past president of the National Cattle Association, has been a favorite to visit. She, along with her daughter's families, is one of the really good folks I've met over the years.

Another place is the Dalebanks Ranch at Eureka. The Perrier family is now moving into their fifth generation of ranching in the same place. They are always interesting to visit, even if you are not in to cattle.

These families, along with folks like the Hinkson family in Chase county, Mark Nikkels of Mill Brae near Alma, and the McCurry family west of Wichita, make up much of what is good in this country. Even though I have an advantage to meet these kind of people, it's possible for almost anybody to have some of the same experiences. Just stop in for breakfast or lunch at any one of hundreds of local restaurants, and join the conversation at the liar's table. Every town or city has those places. The vast majority will welcome you with stories of local color and information. I almost never hesitate to join in and listen.

Driving the side roads, it seems that there are almost always extended vistas and wildlife if you look, as well as a close up look at what feeds our whole nation, the best of anyplace in the world.

Before I forget, I need to mention that there are also many really good places to eat. Kansas City has a bunch of good restaurants if you like steak and barbeque. Many of the small towns have outstanding cafes and small steak houses. All across the state there are blue-plate heavens.

One of my favorite places to visit is Cottonwood Falls. It is cattle country right in the middle of the Flint Hills. Their county agent, Mike Holder, has become a friend over the years. I try never to miss an opportunity to stop for lunch and some good conversation at the Emma Chase Café.

WRAPPING UP

I have now been working on this book about three years. When it was started, I felt that I would have a rough draft finished by Christmas, do some rewrites during the winter, put pictures and side stories in by summer, then try to get at least a fairly finished first copy printed.

When I read *Blue Highways* again, I picked up that Least Heat Moon took five years and multiple rewrites to come up with something he was satisfied with, and he was a trained writer. I think it was just over confidence that led me to believe that I could write something that I would be satisfied with in a year. While a joy, it is also a mentally taxing job. It has become kind of like my house renovation project that I thought would be completed. Maybe, just maybe I can finish before I die.

In writing about my journeys, I realized that I had seen and experienced a lot and have been fortunate to see and experience more than most people. In talking to people about what I was doing and in hearing about their travels, I feel my concepts of what, where, and how varies from the norm. There have been very few conversations where they seem to share my philosophy and preferences about journeys. I think it is mostly because they have never tried it. Those that have traveled with me, whether family, friends, or our cattlemen, seem to have often modified their own travels some, and usually tell me about getting on the gray roads for at least a part of their journey.

The other thing I have picked up is that people rarely really try to interact with the *locals* when they travel. I particularly find this among people younger than me. It seems, in general, that they are quite content to go only to the same places and do the same things and rarely consider anything along the way worth doing or seeing. Most often, it is to a place that is populated only by people like them, doing the same things they are. They have gotten away but taken it with them.

FUTURE DESTINATIONS

I have said before that there will not ever be enough time or money to see and do all I would like. However, I do have some specific places that I sure would like to get to.

For the first time:

1. Alaska—which will mean I have been to all fifty states
2. Newfoundland
3. Camp in the Redwoods

4. Northern Canada to see the Aurora Borealis

5. Yellowstone in winter.

For revisiting:

1. Camp in the Canadian Rockies

2. North Rim of the Grand Canyon

3. Spend several days again in Yellowstone

4. Crater Lake in Oregon

5. Cinnamon Pass in southwest Colorado

Finally, I would really like to sometime make a trip like my parents did in 1968 in the little pop-up Volkswagen Campmobile. We would leave home by May 15 and wander south and west to the Rockies. Then I'd like to go north to Canada, past Edmonton, and west to the coast and down to at least Morro Bay in California, then zigzag my way home across the country, arriving home before frost. On the trip, I'd like to try to not ever travel more than four hours in a day, and stay a few days when we find a place we like.

Recently, it hit me that Diane and I celebrated twenty-five years together in 2009. It has been quite a journey, greatly enriched by what happened along the way. For those twenty-five years she has shared most of my dreams and has been a true soul mate for my journeys. Maybe, just maybe we can fulfill that wish list.

FINISH UP DAMN'IT

Like life, travels can be a continuous journey of awe and wonder, but eventually will come to an end. While no big trips have been done since the writing of the bulk of this story, they continue. But at some point there needs to be a pause, and this is it—enough for now.

A NEW GRAY ROAD!